Rifle and Riflemen

Rifle and Riflemen

Two Works on the Development of Light Troops,
Their Operations & Weapons

A Treatise Upon the Duties of Light Troops

Colonel Von Ehwald

Twenty-Three Years Practice and
Observations with Rifle Guns

Ezekiel Baker

LEONAUR

Rifle and Riflemen
Two Works on the Development of Light Troops, Their Operations & Weapons
A Treatise Upon the Duties of Light Troops by Colonel Von Ehwald
and
Twenty-Three Years Practice and Observations with Rifle Guns by Ezekiel Baker

FIRST EDITION

Leonaur is an imprint of Oakpast Ltd

Copyright in this form © 2011 Oakpast Ltd

ISBN: 978-0-85706-727-2 (hardcover)
ISBN: 978-0-85706-728-9 (softcover)

http://www.leonaur.com

Publisher's Notes

The opinions of the authors represent a view of events in which he
was a participant related from his own perspective,
as such the text is relevant as an historical document.

The views expressed in this book are not necessarily
those of the publisher.

Contents

A Treatise Upon the Duties of Light Troops

Colonel Von Ehwald

Contents

To

FIELD MARSHAL HIS ROYAL HIGHNESS

THE DUKE OF YORK,

COMMANDER IN CHIEF, &C. &C.

THIS TRANSLATION

IS MOST HUMBLY DEDICATED,

WITH

HIS ROYAL PERMISSION,

BY HIS MOST OBEDIENT

AND MOST DEVOTED SERVANT,

A. MAIMBURG,

LATE LIEUT, OF THE 8TH (OR KING'S) REGT. OF INFANTRY.

Preface

The work of Colonel Ehwald upon Light Troops is well known, and highly considered in the military country of Germany. The author served with distinction in the revolutionary war of America, in the Hessian troops in British pay; and has since commanded a light corps in the service of His Danish Majesty.

The excellent precepts which he lays down for the conduct of such troops, in the various circumstances of the *petite guerre*, are exemplified from the celebrated occurrences of the seven years war, the American, and other campaigns.

The application of useful lessons to events which have actually happened, and are extremely interesting, holds them up in a clear point of view to the understanding, and fixes them deep in the memory.

The translator therefore flatters himself that the following Treatise cannot fail to prove useful to the British army.

It has been thought necessary to omit the part of this work which treated of manoeuvres, as they were all old and now no more practiced in Germany; it would only have increased the bulk and price of the volume, and have been likely to mislead young officers: the movements for light infantry, which the author recommends, are all to be found in the Rules and Regulations; and what is peculiar to riflemen, is more in detail in Colonel Rothemburg's work.

The charts of the seven years war, especially that by Moller, of the Wetterau, are recommended by the author to elucidate the examples which he produces for instruction.

CHAPTER 1

Of the Formation of a Light Corps

SECTION 1

In order to obviate the inconveniences which must arise from a want of Light Troops, it would be advantageous for an army that the troops of the line should be instructed to perform the duties of Light Troops.

In a military system where it is wished that light troops should be made less necessary, the only way would be to instruct the troops of the line to perform those particular duties. Armies would then be better secured against attacks from the enemy, and the most arduous enterprises would seldomer fail, than when entrusted to light corps raised generally in a hurry, at the beginning of a war, and composed frequently of the dregs of the human race, upon whom no dependence can be placed on account of the frequent desertions which never fail to happen among them after unsuccessful events, or towards the end of a campaign. Why should not the troops of the line be taught and practise the same duties, being (as they are) made up of the same sort of men, and cloathed and armed alike? the difference of the name alone cannot constitute a different kind of troops.

This duty ought not to be performed by detachments, but by whole regiments, battalions, or squadrons, which should be relieved after two or three months of that harassing duty; the soldier of the line would thereby become more hardy, and what seldom happens to him, except in a battle or engagement, he would often see the enemy, and accustom himself to that fight. Thus, an army would be formed, calculated to cope with any nation, capable of fighting after any manner, and in a pitched battle it would not be deprived of a considerable proportion of its numbers. The officer, who would find in the performance of this duty daily opportunities to distinguish himself and acquire reputation, would eagerly apply to the study of the *petite guerre*. A number of good officers would thus be reared, and the general would no more be at a loss (as it is but too often the case at present) where to find in critical circumstances a field officer equal to a difficult undertaking.

A light company and a light troop might be added to the regiments of infantry and cavalry; the only difference in the arms would be in a rifle with a long bayonet, for the light companies, and the light troops would be mounted upon light horses and wear sabres instead of broad swords; these being lighter, and better calculated for cutting.

The force of these companies can be augmented in time of war, according to circumstances, and formed into battalions or squadrons under the command of field officers qualified for that kind of warfare both by study and experience.

In time of peace, at the season appointed for exercise, these companies are every year to be formed into battalions, as is the case with the grenadier companies in Germany; are to be commanded by capable field officers, and uniformly instructed; the inspection of the whole must be intrusted to one of these field officers. During the season of exercise an example of all the different occurrences which can happen in war must be practised for the instruction of officers and non-commissioned officers; for instance, how an advance, or rear guard, or a *patrole* is to be conducted; how to act on a reconnoitring party; how to make a report of what they have been *ordered* to perform; in what manner to take post with a detachment of infantry or cavalry; how to fortify a post in a short time, and how to cover it by videttes and centinels, how these must be placed, and when the detachment is too weak to supply as many sentries as the ground requires, in what manner it can be secured against surprise by *patroles*.

Officers and non-commissioned officers must receive clear instructions concerning attacks by surprise and ambuscades, in what manner to attack, or carry a post by a *coup de main*, how to defend or attack a village, how to make loop-holes in a wall, how to fix a petard to a gate (every officer ought to know how it is to be managed); they must be taught how to find their way in an unknown country, and what is the best manner of becoming acquainted with the nature of a country; how to judge with accuracy of the distance and number of troops, how to take every advantage against the enemy, and to practise all the stratagems of war. How advantageous it would be for an army to have a body of light troops formed in this manner! 200 of them, under an able commander would perform what in general requires a thousand; however inconsiderable their number, such troops would no doubt look without fear upon a superior number of raw and undisciplined soldiers, for superiority over an enemy in the field is acquired rather by the quality than the number of men. The Swedes under Charles XII. and the Prussians in the seven years war have proved the truth of this assertion.

The greatest attention must be paid to complete these light companies at the end of a campaign, not with deserters or raw recruits, but by drafts from the regiments of hardy and well made young lads, not less than 5 feet 4 inches high, as it is practiced in the British light companies, and in France in the *chasseur* companies.

Regiments of hussars or light dragoons have indeed been raised in every country, in order to have a permanent light cavalry; and battalions of light infantry and riflemen have lately been placed upon the regular establishment, for the sake of having, at the beginning of a war, a number of light troops ready formed; but these do not answer the purpose, since they do not consist entirely of trusty men, upon whose faith the most implicit confidence can be placed; besides, the number of such light troops is not proportionate to the force of our present large armies in time of war; therefore, new corps of that description must be raised at the beginning of a war.

I shall now proceed to deliver my ideas upon the composition which will render a light corps serviceable in war, and upon the kind of instruction necessary for it; I shall also point out how its commander and officers are to act in every circumstance.

Section 2
Qualifications of Officers; of Recruitings and Discipline.

In levying such corps the commander ought never to be suffered to sell his companies or other commissions, or to dispose of them for a certain number of recruits; for if he be of a covetous disposition, he will certainly sacrifice the good of the service to his private interest.

The absolute necessity of light troops is universally acknowledged; the safety of an army rests upon them; they are necessary to its very existence. Experience proves that an army provided with a sufficient body of these troops under the command of able and enterprising leaders, enjoys perfect security in its camp, while another deficient in that respect is constantly alarmed and teazed on every side, besieged in its own camp, and when on a march is perpetually harassed by the enemy. However convinced of all this, as everybody is, yet no attention is paid to the choice of officers for these corps; profligate and abandoned men are frequently appointed to them, who, by their vices, ignorance, and indolence, must at last ruin the reputation of the corps, while, in fact, they ought to be extremely nice about the moral character of officers, and careful to admit none who are addicted to drinking, gambling, or women; and indeed how could a man, whose spirits are exhausted by such vicious habits, support the fatigues of war, and be always vigilant and alert.

Indeed military experience alone can give an idea of all the qualifications necessary to render an officer fit to serve in the light troops. He is always in presence of the enemy; the most imminent danger must never make the least impression upon him; he must always remain cool and capable of profiting by every circumstance or fault which the enemy may commit; what the general does upon a large scale, he must do upon a small one; how could he indeed, separated from the army and left to himself, receive directions from the general upon his conduct, and how could the general give him such directions as would apply to every occurrence, when circumstances may change every moment? Should he be thus circumscribed, how often would he lose the opportunity of executing some lucky *coup de main*, or perhaps fall into faults which might be attended with the most serious consequences for the army? How many instances could be produced, where the ignorance or neglect of the commander of an outpost, or reconnoitring party, has been attended with the ruin of armies and the loss of whole provinces? nay, I will maintain that the carelessness and unskilfulness of an officer of *yägers* (who, fortunately for himself, lost his life eight days after), had been the cause of the irreparable loss of fourteen provinces; had this officer sent reconnoitring parties up the banks of the Delaware, as he ought to have done, the approach of General Washington must have been discovered, and the attack of Trainton would have proved fatal to the Americans.

I flatter myself to have clearly proved the necessity of appointing able officers to the light troops; in short, these corps require the cleanest, best behaved, trustiest, most active, capable and brave officers, who joyfully embrace this kind of warfare, despising danger, renouncing ease and comfort, and submitting with pleasure to the fatigues and hardships of war.

The commander of such a corps can, therefore, never be too strict; he must from the first day of its formation communicate his intentions to the officers, that he will be happy to find opportunities of serving them, but that in the meantime he requests their implicit obedience to his orders, in return for which he will place the greatest confidence in them; he must represent to them how necessary it is that the efforts of everyone should be applied to the common advantage; he must, from the first moment, take notice of the most trifling irregularity; he will give strict orders to the officers that they are never to be absent from their companies without his leave, and he will never permit any to be absent a minute from exercise. He will give them to understand that they are henceforth to consider the corps as their home, and to look upon their duties as their only pastime and amusement. He is never to suffer any rioting or gambling among them, for their future conduct will depend much upon the lessons which they receive at first.

Such a commander must also act as liberally with his officers as his circumstances will admit; he must invite them often to his table, to have opportunities to become acquainted with their disposition, and to gain their confidence; but he ought to behave with decorum, and avoid that familiarity which too much wine occasions, and which always ends in contempt. He must try to correct, or at least conceal his faults, so as not to lose the respect which is due to him. Is he obliged to punish an officer? he must be very cautious not to offend him by harsh language, for nothing can be more distressing to a man of honour than to be hurt in his feelings by one from whom he cannot demand satisfaction; he will in this case assure the officer whom he is obliged to punish, that he is very sorry to be under that necessity, and hopes it will be the first and last time; he must always show the greatest impartiality in his punishments, as a contrary conduct is sure to create hatred; all his actions must in fact be calculated to obtain the love of his officers, and make them consider themselves as happy to be under his command.

It will also be necessary at the formation of such a corps to get from the line a proportion of trusty non-commissioned officers and men, in order to forward the instruction of the recruits; but these draughts ought to consist of faithful, active, and brave young men, and none of those old, worn out, ill-behaved and ill-natured fellows, as is in general the case; because the regiments of the line seize such opportunities to get rid of their worst men. At the formation of such a corps the commander ought also to pay some attention to the kind of recruits, and not admit improper subjects in order to be completed a little sooner.

If the circumstances admit of being nice in the choice of men, it will be proper to pay attention to the profession of the recruits that offer, as well as to their age and size; no printers, bookbinders, taylors, shoemakers, or weavers, should be enlisted, as from their business they contrast habits of effeminacy, and are unable to support the fatigues of war; none should be received who are under 5 feet 4 inches high, or above 30 years of age; between 16 and 30 man is in the bloom of life, and fit to endure all the hardships of war, and when it comes to close quarters a well-proportioned man from 5 feet 7 to 10 inches is preferable to one of a less size, because he can reach farther with his weapons.

Old soldiers are not to be sought after: I was persuaded of the contrary when I raised in the Hessian service one of the two first rifle companies which were to serve in America; but how soon was I made sensible of my mistake in the first campaign; the young men stood perfectly the climate and every hardship, while the old soldiers, whose constitution had already been impaired by former campaigns, were soon laid up, and sent to the hospital, and I remarked also that young men were more to be depended upon either in attack or defence; for being engaged with my company for the first time the day after our landing in the province of New York, I had the misfortune while reconnoitring to be completely surrounded by a far superior number of riflemen; my old soldiers were the first who perceived our situation, and I was forsaken by many of them, but the young lads stood by me in the innocence of their hearts, and to them I owed the preservation of myself and my party excepting two who were taken prisoners.

The severest discipline must be established in such a corps from the first moment; for a commanding officer can never be too strict with men collected from all corners of the world; no fault, however trifling, ought to be overlooked.

When men are accustomed to strict discipline, punishment becomes less necessary. Rewards and punishments in such corps must be in the extreme; those who behave well or distinguish themselves must be publicly praised and encouraged by rewards and promotion, the disobedient must be punished in the most exemplary manner; especially such as are not watchful on duty, drunkards, gamblers, and plunderers, who rob and use ill the inhabitants of the country.

The best way with such hardened sinners would be, after conviction of their crimes, to strip them naked to the shirt, shave their heads, and turn them out in the most shameful manner before the front of the whole corps; punishments of this sort make a deeper impression than the severest corporal ones; I was only once obliged to use it, before our departure for America, and the effect was such that for some time after, I had no punishment at all to inflict.

It is an error to believe that you will gain the love of the soldiers by showing a culpable indulgence to them at the expence of the poor peasants, who have already too much to suffer from war; by no means! The soldier will try everything, if a crime be once overlooked, he will trust to your weakness, and excesses of every kind will grow so frequent that the honour of the corps and the corps itself must be ruined; the enraged inhabitants of the country, in order to revenge their sufferings, will seize every opportunity to betray you to the enemy, and this alone may be attended with the most serious consequences, while by discipline and good behaviour friends may be made even in an enemy's country.

Before I conclude this section, I shall propose a method which will perhaps be found the best, to put a stop to desertion, which is in general so frequent with such corps, and is not considered as seriously as it ought to be. A deserter is pardoned after going over to the enemy two of three times with his arms and accoutrements, of which he has robbed his sovereign or his captain, and he is received with pleasure if he bring with him other arms from the enemy; nay, I have known an instance where a sentry deserting from his post was pardoned because he came back, when if the enemy had profited by the circumstance it would have been the ruin of the corps, and perhaps of the whole army.

With men who have enlisted of their own accord, commanding officers have of course an undoubted right to punish desertion severely, which may prove of the most dangerous consequence at outposts. In my opinion this practise (so frequent with light troops that nothing is thought of it) could be easily stopped by marking a gallows upon the foreheads of such as are caught, with a red hot iron, and then sending them back to the enemy; the fear of infamy will more effectually prevent crimes than that of death; this punishment may also be used against those who are guilty of barbarity towards the country people, of which I could relate such shocking instances, that it would make every friend of humanity shudder, and would disgrace human nature.

Notwithstanding the severity of discipline, you should convince the soldiers that you love them; the greatest care must be taken to procure for them punctually what they have a right to expect, and that they never suffer from the selfishness of their captain (which must be severely punished), they must feel that they are suffered to enjoy all the good which can be allowed them, and the commanding officer must show himself perfectly disinterested in all his transactions; by such conduct he will find himself able to execute anything with his men, and if by his good behaviour, address, and courage he has once gained the confidence of his inferiors, he may depend upon them in all situations; but he must not permit grumbling either among officers or soldiers, however harassing the duty may be.

Section 3
Of the Strength of a Light Corps

In order to render such a corps useful, it must be composed of infantry and cavalry, as the mutual support of these two arms greatly increases their strength.

Such a corps ought not to be under 1200 or at least 1000 strong, but it would be a fault, on the other side, to make it much stronger, for instance to augment it to 2 or 3 thousand; because officers, capable of leading such corps, as they ought to be, are rare in any army; but should it be less numerous than we have proposed, it would be impossible for its commander to perform important and brilliant actions, because such a corps, being daily engaged with the enemy, must of course get weaker every day, and should it by any unfortunate accident suffer a considerable loss, it would at once be made incapable of serving actively for the remainder of the campaign.

I have seen during the American war that several British light corps of 6 or 700 men, were, at the end of a fatiguing campaign, reduced to less than half their number actually under arms; and my own experience has shown me, that a detachment of which I had the command in the campaign in Virginia, consisting of 125 riflemen, the two flank companies of an English regiment of 50 men each and 30 horse, was, at the end of the campaign, reduced to 60 men fit for service; and out of the 125 Hessian and Anspach riflemen I could muster no more than 20 under arms on the day that York town capitulated. This will prove the impropriety of sending weak corps or detachments to a distance from the army, where they cannot be relieved.

The half or at least a third must be cavalry; so that something may be undertaken with it alone, if that be found necessary. It would also be advantageous if the infantry of a light corps were mounted; small and strong horses of a low price might be bought for them. Their appearance and use would then be the same as that of dragoons at their first establishment, when it was intended to remove expeditiously the flower of the infantry from one place to another.

What is in fact the use of a light corps but to move rapidly, to find out the enemy and teasing him to night in one place, get the distance of ten or twelve leagues from him by next morning? Thus cavalry would never be obliged to act without its infantry in a *coup de main*, which requires expedition, and such a corps would be able to undertake anything, and especially in an uneven and woody country could constantly and unexpectedly harass the enemy in every direction. If threatened by a superior force, such a corps could escape by the rapidity of its motions, and in order to save the cavalry, the infantry would never be sacrificed to the enemy; it could cross any river, and might attempt to carry even fortified towns of the second order.

I shall introduce here a sketch of the formation of such a corp.

Two companies of foot riflemen, each composed of:
1 Captain,
1 First Lieutenant,
2 Second Lieutenants,
2 Bugle horns,
20 Non-commissioned officers; called *overjagers*, the most capable among them will have charge of the Company's Roster, another will be Fourier,[1] and a third Captain of Arms,
200 Privates.

Thus 10 men will form a squad, the force of the company will be 226, and both companies 452 strong. Such a company can perform a great deal of actual service before it grows so weak as to be incapable of acting with efficacy. The eldest captain of the two ought to be of known capacity and courage.

Two companies of light infantry:
1 Captain,
1 First Lieutenant,
2 Second Lieutenants,
1 Sergeant,
1 Captain of Arms
16 Corporals,
2 Bugle horns, (whom I would give also to these light companies, in order to accustom the whole corps to obey the sounds,

---

1. The employment of Fourier answers to that of pay sergeant.

as well as the voice, and because this instrument is preferable to any other in the field, as it may be distinctly heard at the distance of three miles) and—
200 Privates.
The whole of the light infantry would thus be 304.

Two squadrons of light horse:
1 Captain,
1 First Lieutenant,
3 Second Lieutenants,
3 Trumpeters,
3 Serjeants,
1 Quarter Master,
16 Corporals,
200 Privates.
The two squadrons 456 effective.

The commander and two field officers are enough for such a corps, but one of the latter ought to have previously served in the cavalry in order to take the command of the two squadrons. For although a good officer, who has sufficiently studied his profession, will certainly be able to lead in a proper manner both infantry and cavalry; yet the interior duties cannot be perfectly known in their *detail* but by an officer who has served in both. The officers of the two squadrons ought to have served in the cavalry, and the officers of the four companies in the infantry, that the men may be properly trained, and the interior duty punctually attended to.

By adding to the corps an auditeur,[2] a clergyman, a quarter master, a surgeon and 6 mates, a waggon master, a gun-smith, a farrier, who must understand the veterinary art, a bugle horn major, a provost, and six good carpenters, who will prove very useful in the fortifying of a post, the whole corps will muster 1381.

It will be very important to procure proper surgeon's mates; and the surgeon himself must be not only a man of professional respectability, but humane and zealous; as through the want of such qualifications many a good soldier who happens to be wounded may lose his limbs or life. And it is to be wished that the sovereign would at the end of a war allow to the regimental surgeons, and physicians of the military hospitals, a certain sum for every man either severely wounded or dangerously ill, whose limbs, health, or life have been preserved by

2. The charge of an auditeur answers to that of judge advocate.

their skill and attention; it would be an encouragement to them, and probably save many a poor soldier. The sovereign would be amply recompensed for this additional expense by the preservation of his subjects and of his brave soldiers.

With regard to the pay of these corps, I have to observe, that the riflemen and the light infantry, as well as the light horse, ought to receive the same; they live and act together, and a difference of pay in the same corps, creates only discontent.

SECTION 4
OF THE CLOTHING AND ARMS OF A LIGHT CORPS.

Green is undoubtedly the best and most convenient colour for light troops, as it is less seen at a distance, and not at all in woods. If I had the choice of the clothing and equipment of such a corps, I would give them a green jacket with black capes and cuffs, it should be made to button the whole length of the body; a green waistcoat with sleeves, calculated to do duty in during the summer.—This dress, with a little repair, might serve for two years, as the soldier would not wear his coat more than sixteen months during that period.

Instead of breeches I would make use of the English trowsers, which answer at once the purpose of breeches and gaiters; only I would have them made sufficiently wide about the calf of the leg and the knee to allow the man to march with ease; this would save the expense of stockings; and thus the soldier will have less to carry in his knapsack, besides the saving of garters and knee buckles, two very inconvenient articles, especially when the men must remain dressed day and night. Trowsers of grey linen ought to be worn in summer, and grey cloth in winter.

For head dress I would recommend a plain well cocked hat with a cockade. Many give the preference to a round hat, but I am not of that opinion; because round hats are more liable to be blown off by the wind, and give a robber-like appearance to the soldier: besides in rainy weather the men pull them so low over their ears, that they become very improper for sentries. I remember upon this subject, that in the first campaign, in the province of Jersey during the American war, as I was on a *patrole*, with the then Captain Von Wraeden, we met, in very rainy and windy weather, with a party of Americans; their advanced guard had their faces so concealed under their round hats, that they never perceived our advanced guard before they were seized by them and made prisoners. Since that time I have been thoroughly

25

convinced that the soldier ought to preserve his sight free; and if it rain very hard, he can let down the back flap of his hat, and thus keep his head and neck dry.

As light troops are not allowed to have tents, and are constantly exposed to the weather, it is proper to give a great coat or blanket to every man in the corps to cover himself with during the night; in rainy or very cold weather he can use the blanket as a great coat; on a march or on sentry it will also be of service to preserve his firelock from the wet.

A rifleman is armed with a rifle, a short cutlass supported by a black or brown belt worn across the shoulders; and a pouch with a belt of the same colour as the first.

The light infantry companies must be provided with good musquets, triangular bayonets, and a pouch as the riflemen. I would not give them side arms, as superfluous for a man who must fight with his bayonet; they are besides inconvenient for marching, augment the expense, and are dangerous in quarrels.

Both squadrons of cavalry must be mounted and armed as light as hussars, with the only difference of a light musquet and a long bayonet instead of a carbine, so that they may be able to fight on foot if necessary.

There ought to be in each squadron twenty-five good shots armed with rifles instead of musquets, they will prove very useful on advance and rear guards, or skirmishes; they can also be used to great advantage when a post or passage must be expeditiously carried by cavalry, and requires to be obstinately defended.

Every squad, of ten men and a corporal in the cavalry, as well as the infantry, ought to carry constantly with them 3 shovels, 2 pickaxes, an axe, and 2 hatchets; in order to be always able to fortify a post when necessary.

Many sensible men are of opinion, that such corps ought to have some light field pieces; but I will maintain, that as the success of the operations of these troops depends upon the rapidity of their movements, artillery would be more cumbersome than useful. I would rather recommend a few petards to be carried, which are better adapted to knock down gates or old walls than two pounders, and can be easily transported upon *bât* horses, in the most rugged country. I shall hereafter treat fully of this, instrument, and acquaint young officers with its use and management.

SECTION 5
OF THE BAGGAGE OF A LIGHT CORPS.

Although light corps ought to have less baggage than others, it will be found that the contrary practice has prevailed among them; for by frequent captures from the enemy, the officers can procure horses and other articles much easier and cheaper than those of other corps, and the quantity of superfluous horses and servants, which they keep, will frequently oblige them to quit a post for want of provisions and forage.

For my part I cannot conceive how generals permit the officers of their armies to have such a monstrous number of servants and horses. If this abuse were corrected, how much longer would an army be able to keep the field! How often has a corps or an army been obliged to quit the best position, through want of forage by taking from these gentlemen the opportunity of diverting themselves with riding, they would be obliged to look to their corps or regiment for amusement; it would also diminish the inconvenience resulting from the extravagant quantity of baggage, which takes away so many men from their duty; for as officers cannot maintain so many servants as the quantity of their baggage requires, they must employ soldiers for this purpose; a field officer will sometimes take three or four, a captain two at least, and the subaltern one, to attend upon their baggage.

Let us reckon at the rate of six or eight men from each company, and we shall see that the general will thereby have several thousand men less on the day of battle; it is also to be remarked that the men employed by the officers are in general the best and trustiest; and to have 2000 of the best soldiers more or less on the day of action is certainly no trifling matter.

Another abuse will also result from the first, namely, that a captain will frequently promote to the rank of non-commissioned officers those men who have served him faithfully; I have even seen people of that description made officers to the great injury of the service; for as such men have frequently, during whole years, had nothing to do but to attend upon the captain, they know nothing about duty, and thus the regiment or corps is filled with the worst non-commissioned officers, who are not respected by the soldier: and the best men seeing by such injustice that good conduct is no recommendation, become discontented and disheartened. Why should not an officer, who is well fed, whose dress is light, and who carries nothing about him but his sword, have as much strength as the common soldier and be as able as he to perform a march upon his feet? consider also, that those among the officers who are fond of shooting, will, for whole days together, remain on their legs, and endure, without complaining, the hardships inseparable from that diversion, but to march with the regiment, that they cannot. And why? because it is not customary.

In the wars in America who gives horses to the English and French officers? From the colonel downwards every one must perform his duty on foot. I have heard Sir William Howe say frequently, that during the seven years war while he commanded, as a colonel, the British light infantry in America, he had always carried himself his own blanket and canteen, and marched on foot My own experience has taught me, during the American war, that an officer can live without horses, and all this depends upon prejudice or custom; it was thought very hard at first and even disgraceful for an officer; I was myself of that opinion, but as it could not be otherwise, we were forced to submit, and by degrees attached our pride to marching on foot, as well as the common soldier.

During the whole American war, I recollect only one officer who actually died of extreme fatigue on a march exposed to the burning sun; while I have seen a great number of men lose their lives in that manner: from which it may be easily concluded, that the officer who fares better and has not overstrained his strength in his youth is able to support more hardships than the common soldier. As this would be advantageous to the sovereign, he could give the officers their rations in money, that they might not suffer by this regulation, for their pay in every country is so low as not to admit of reduction.

I will point out here the quantity of baggage which a light corps ought to have, and which would be sufficient for any part of the globe.

Commanding officer, 2 saddle and 2 servants' horses, 2 *bât* horses, a servant, a cook, a groom, and a *bât* man.
The field officer of the cavalry,—2 saddle horses, 1 for a servant, 2 *bât* horses, a servant, a groom and *bât* man.
The captain of a troop,—2 saddle horses, a servant's and a *bât* horse, a servant, a groom, and *bât* man.
For a lieutenant,—2 saddle horses.
The four officers of each squadron,—2 mounted valets, and 2 *bât* horses and *bât* men.

The field officer of the infantry,—2 saddle horses, 1 for a servant, and 2 *bât* horses, a valet, a servant, and a *bât* man.

The captain of a company,—a saddlehorse, a *bât* horse, a servant, and *bât* man.

The first lieutenant is allowed the same; and the two sub-lieutenants,—2 saddle horses, a *bât* horse, and 2 valets.

The auditeur and clergyman,—-2 saddle horses, and a *bât* horse.

The surgeon and quartermaster have each, a saddle and a *bât* horse, and a servant and valet; 2 *bât* horses more are allowed for medicine chests. The waggon master, a saddle horse; and the farrier, a cart with one horse, supplied by the sovereign.

Beside these horses, the sovereign may allow to each company a *bât* horse and *bât* man, to afford an opportunity to the officers commanding companies of carrying a few spare arms and shoes or boots; besides a cart with two horses for readymade cartridges. To prevent any abuse, the charge of this cart and company *bât* horses must be given to the waggon master. As light troops have no tents, of course officers must not be allowed to have any tent or field bed; a bear or deer skin, or a blanket besides the great coat must suffice.

No officer in the Hessian and Anspach *yägers*, during the whole of the American war, ever carried with him any tent, or bed, table or chair; and once used to it we did not dislike this hard way of living; and I do not believe that upon an average we had more sick officers than the regulars. But the commander must be the first to give a good example; and above all the greatest attention must be paid to allow the soldier to carry in his knapsack as little as possible. A shirt, a green foraging cap, one pair of stockings, and a few brushes are sufficient. The knapsacks ought to be inspected every week, and everything superfluous indiscriminately burnt. But the time for being strictest is when the men have got booty from the enemy; you must insist upon their selling off the whole instantly, or else they will load themselves like beasts of burthen, and be incapable of following the corps.

Chapter 2

Drilling and Manoeuvres

Section 1
Of the Manual Exercise for Light Infantry and Cavalry.

Light corps are in general found to be indifferently drilled, and to understand nothing of manoeuvres; their movements are not correct; nay, I have seen several which were hardly able to face to the right or left about, or march by sections.

The principal cause of this evil is, that these corps are frequently raised in too great an hurry, and that an improper method is followed at first. The instruction begins according to custom where it ought to end.

The whole attention is turned to a useless handling of arms and to trifles, while what is truly useful to such a corps is forgotten. The corps is completed, the inspector indulgent, and the muster is passed; it then proceeds to the army, where it first begins to see its defects.

There are men who pretend to be acquainted with military matters, and who, while they are ignorant of the method of training light troops, call everything of this nature useless pedantry. They say that in presence of the enemy all these school rules fall to the ground; that as light troops must carry everything sword in hand, or with charged bayonets, why should they be tormented for nothing!

But these good folks do not consider that to attack an enemy in that manner, a battalion or squadron must have been previously well disciplined, since the force of their shock depends upon good order and compactness. From this false principle attacks and ambuscades are frequently unsuccessful, and the confusion arises which prevails so often in rear-guards, occasioning a severe loss, and degenerating sometimes into a complete rout Many people falsely imagine, that drill and exercise are not necessary for light troops, because they never are obliged to fight a pitched battle in close order; however, supposing that a light corps, of which I have seen examples during the American war, should have the good fortune to escape the bad consequences which may attend want of proper instruction; yet surely it would be more satisfactory for a commander, and better deserve the approbation of men of sense, if he were to discipline his corps so as to be calculated for all sorts of duties; besides, it looks well, and impresses even the enemy with a certain respect, when the appearance and discipline of a light corps are equal to that of a regiment of the line. The soldier himself feels a certain confidence and pride from the consciousness of his skill, and is prepared for everything.

There is also another kind of persons, who are appointed to light corps, because they understand drilling; such are of opinion, that when the soldier is taught to handle smartly his firelock, march well on the parade, and kneel briskly, the object is obtained, and the science of war exhausted. These people exercise the whole day, torment the poor soldier until the moment for taking the field arrives, and then the whole science of the commander and his officers consists in the knowledge of marching and the manual exercise. Believe me, it is not everyone who is qualified for instructing a light corps in a proper manner, and is able to lead, it in the field; a commander must have been brought up to it, and have been formed by campaigns.

The great master in the art of war saw that light troops must be kept on the peace establishment, in order to form them, and make the most of them in war. This great king raised a proportionate number of regiments of hussars, augmented the *yäger* corps to two battalions, and a short time before his death, he formed several light infantry regiments: his royal successor followed the same plan, and increased the light infantry to 20 battalions; these are well officered, and have men of talents and experience at their head. Several powers have lately followed the example, augmented their hussars, and placed *yäger* battalions upon their establishment, of which they will find the advantage at the first war.

The recruits must be appointed to the companies as soon as enlisted, and begin the drill immediately, that they may not remain too long idle in the recruiting districts.

As soon as the recruit can face to his right and left, let him march and wheel for a few days in ranks, without arms; after which, you will put the firelock into his hands, teach him the necessary motions, to prime, load, and fire, and practise him to fire at the target. You divide the companies into two or three platoons, and practise together those who have made equal progress. The corps may be complete in its exercise in the space of six weeks, if the officers and non-commissioned officers do their duty, by drilling twice a day, three hours at a time; and when the men are perfect in the manual, by devoting the morning to fire at the target, and the afternoon to exercise and manoeuvres.

The cleanliness of the soldier must also be attended to; for it is necessary to his comfort and health; and even in the field, when labouring under the greatest hardships, when a minute can be spared, the men must be ordered to wash, comb their heads, and shift. It must not be thought that it is impossible to keep the soldier clean during a hard campaign; there is nothing impossible! give your orders, support them with firmness, and you will see every obstacle vanish; it was the favourite principle of Colonel Donop, who fell at Redbank in America, and he never was disappointed in the application of it. The Hessian brigade of grenadiers occupied a winter cantonment in New Brunswick at the beginning of 1777; they were kept in constant alarm by the Americans, who had become very bold since the affair of Trainton, and were obliged to stand by their arms day and night without taking off their clothes.

The brigade was quartered by companies in wretched and half ruined houses, and had hardly straw to lay upon; however, the cleanliness of the Hessian grenadiers when they came upon duty, was such as to attract the notice of the English themselves, who are naturally very clean, and excel all other polished nations in this respect. Nobody knows what the soldier may be used to; accustom him to what is right, and you will obtain everything from him. During the American war, the detachments and detached corps were for a whole campaign without women, and for whole months with only the shirt they had upon their backs. The English soldiers used to wash their shirts themselves, dried them expeditiously, and put them on again; the German soldiers saw it, and followed the example. We were soon persuaded, that our linen could be washed without women, and many of our soldiers continued the same practice afterwards, when they found that it saved their purse.

Before I proceed farther, I must say, that, in my opinion, the infantry of a light corps ought to be in two ranks; for, as these corps are frequently single-handed against the enemy, it will encrease the front, and it is easier to march in line in two than three ranks through woods and bushes; and the firing by ranks, which I have adopted, can be as well practiced in two as three ranks. In an attack with charged bayonets, I am convinced, that if the corps drawn up in two ranks advances resolutely upon the other in three, it will not be worse off for that rank less, as the pressure of one upon the other, of which the French tacticians speak, exists only in the imagination.

If it were in my power, I would place the shortest men in the front, and the tallest in the second rank, because both will fire with more ease; and in an attack with the bayonet, the effect of this weapon would be greater, as, what is lost in this case, by the distance of the second rank, would be gained by their superior size and the length of their arms; but if you place the smallest men in the second rank, their bayonets cannot do much execution, and those of the third, none at all, any more than the third rank in the cavalry. The American inspector general, Van Steuben, introduced this practice in General Washington's army, and, in spite of custom and prejudice, I did not find it gave a bad appearance; besides, utility ought to be the first recommendation in war.

Section 2
Of Flanking, or Acting in Open Order, or en Tirailleur

When a certain number of light infantry or light horse fights dispersed, it is called flanking skirmishing, or acting *en tirailleur*. This kind of fighting requires more training than any other, as the light horse or *yäger* is generally left to himself, and must follow his own judgement. Frequent use of calls must be made, and the men well practiced to obey them, as given with the trumpet, bugle, or drum. They must also be taught to extend briskly, form a kind of chain, or a half circle, and to occupy without delay the whole of such ground as may be advantageous, or which has been pointed out to them. They must know how to outflank the enemy's *tirailleurs*, and be so alert and collected, that Should a single flanker of the enemy separate from his party, he must at the same instant be killed or made prisoner; and as they frequently engage singly, their bravery must sometimes be temerity, and they must be good shots, in order to command the respect of the enemy. For these reasons, every *yäger* cannot be employed in this kind of duty, and the officers commanding companies must of course endeavour to know among their men such as are fit for it.

Companies must be divided into sections of flankers, according to individual merit; for instance, the bravest and fittest non-commissioned officers and men will be called first flankers, the best after them are called second, and the lowest class will be the third. Although *yägers* be thus picked out for this kind of duty, every *yäger* must nevertheless be taught to perform it, as in war it frequently happens, that whole companies and whole corps must be employed to skirmish, as in reconnoitring, or to conceal a manoeuvre from the enemy.

SECTION 3
OF RETREATING.

A retreat can be performed either in line by the whole corps, the light infantry in the centre, riflemen on both wings, every platoon having its proportion of flankers detached to the rear and flanks, to cover the line, and skirmish during the retreat; or by platoons retiring *en echequier*, those which have to make head against the enemy, will also send out their flankers to skirmish with the enemy, and cover the retreat. In the first instance, flankers must be relieved every hour, for neither the men nor their muskets could stand it much longer, if the pursuit be close and obstinate. They should be relieved in the following manner; every platoon must be previously divided into three or four sections; when the first is to be relieved, the men must be cautioned, that at the word *flankers' relief*, the second section must instantly extend, and relieve individually every man of the first section, observing not to stop the retreat in performing the relief, but proceed in the meantime; when the flankers of the first section see that their places are occupied, they retire slowly to their platoons, and form into section again.

In the second instance, the platoons which are to make head against the enemy, will relieve the flankers of the retreating platoons, at the distance of 200 or 300 paces, and the flankers of the retreating platoons must not fall in into their platoons, but a short distance before the spot where it will be the turn of these platoons to make head again. The distance between these two lines must depend upon circumstances and upon the ground, the usual distance is 300 paces. If the flankers be overpowered, they must be instantly supported by another section, especially those on the flanks, who are most exposed, and who must be very cautious, that the enemy do not outflank and cut them off. To prevent this, they ought always to form a half circle round each flank. Every company sends an officer, and every section a non-commissioned officer to the skirmishers; each line a captain, who must be on horseback in the field. In a retreat in line, a captain and three subalterns must be commanded for skirmishing.

In a woody and bushy country, the best way will be to retire by alternate files, without flankers, and it can be performed in the best order.

Section 4
Of Cavalry.

Having been bred in the infantry, I am not therefore sufficiently conversant with this arm to treat of its details in a satisfactory manner, I must content myself with pointing out its principal duties.

Whatever a light dragoon has to perform on horseback, he must be taught on foot; after which, he must learn to mount and dismount from his horse in a regular manner, to keep erect and firm upon his saddle, how to rise in his stirrups, and cut the enemy: he must also be instructed to cut at a post with the sabre, and to fire with pistols in trotting and galloping. Cavalry must be frequently practiced to wheel by four, by half squadrons, and whole squadrons. Frequent charges of 2000 paces ought to be made in full gallop, and the word of command, *halt!* be given unexpectedly, in order to see whether the men be attentive, and can manage their horses. They must also be taught to saddle and fall in quickly and in good order, in case of alarm, or after having acted as skirmishers.

The riflemen of each squadron must be taught to fire true on horseback, and on that account ought to have the best and quieted horses.

All the movements of a light corps, either infantry or cavalry, must be regulated by the military instruments, and the men frequently practised to the different beatings or tunes, in order to prevent officers and non-commissioned officers from being obliged to *halloo* to the men, and make a great noise, which must occasion confusion, when circumstances require that no time should be lost, and success often depends upon seizing the favourable moment

Should the corps be raised in the neighbourhood of a navigable river or of a sea port, it would be highly proper to practise the men to embark in boats and land, for confusion and frequent accidents are sure to take place in this case, with troops that have not been used to it. This is in general entrusted to sea officers, who care very little how the men get into the boats, so as there be the proper number, which creates such a confusion on landing, that much time is lost, before a few thousand men can form properly. Great attention must be paid when embarking, that the men observe the strictest silence; they must step into the boats by files, and remain there in the same order as in the ranks, in order that at the moment of landing they may spring out by files, and form in succession on the left of the first. Should the embarkation take place in the night, the greatest care will be required to prevent confusion.

With cavalry it is to be observed, that the men must be prevented from obstructing each other; when the first man leads his horse into the boat, he must instantly take post before him, the second man does the same to the left of the first, the third man follows the first, and the fourth follows the second, and so on till the boat be full. As a flat-bottomed boat does not in general carry more than 40 or 50 men, or 8 or 10 horses, every officer commanding a company ought to take care that the boats which have his company on board keep together, in order that they may land at the same place. This ought to be principally attended to with infantry, as it may happen that they have to land in face of the enemy.

Cavalry must be used to ride their horses into the boats, and to alight there, and lead them to the appointed place; when horses are once used to it, the embarkation is soon performed.

The cavalry of our army in Virginia had become so perfect in embarking and disembarking, by daily occasions on our marches of passing the navigable rivers by which that country is so much intersected, and by our frequent expeditions upon the water, that it was astonishing how expeditiously and regularly they could perform it.

I saw an example of the contrary while a prisoner. Two or three hundred of the French hussars of the *legion de Lauzun* had to cross over York River, by Gloucester, after the surrender of York, and spent the whole day before they could get over.

As soon as the corps is capable of manoeuvring sufficiently, instead of marching straight to and from the place of exercise, it ought to be manoeuvred all the way, that no time may be lost.

All the different manners of breaking and forming ought to be practiced, and the corps never go out without detaching advance and rear guards, and lateral *patroles*, and seizing that opportunity of instructing the officers and non-commissioned officers how to perform these duties in the field.

The duty of the field ought to be introduced in quarters. The place may be occupied in the same manner as if the enemy were near, an alarm post fixed, and officers and non-commissioned officers taught how to make a *patrole*. False alarms must now and then be given, both day and night, in order to practise the men to fall in expeditiously and in good order. In fact, the commander of the corps must endeavour to give it general notions of the duties of the fields that the officers and non-commissioned officers may be in some degree prepared upon the most important points, previously to their taking the fields

CHAPTER 3

Of the Duty of an Officer of Light Infantry

SECTION 1
HOW AN OFFICER OF LIGHT INFANTRY OUGHT TO ACT UPON A MARCH.

Before I treat of the duty of a commander of a light corps in the field, I will mention the most important particulars in the duty of an officer of light infantry and cavalry, for how often does it happen in war, that an officer must act according to his own judgement? He may be sent out on *patrole*, or on a long and dangerous march, in order to occupy a post, or relieve another: he may be sent out with lateral *patroles*, advance and rear guards.

Before an officer goes off with his detachment, he ought to see if the soldiers have loaded their arms, and if in good order; whether their flints are fast and well screwed, their cartridges good and properly arranged in the pouch, for this, as I have experienced myself, is often neglected, therefore an officer cannot be too attentive to this abuse. As soon as he begins his march, he ought to keep his detachment together in the greatest order, command his men to be silent, and allow none, except in the greatest emergency, to fall out of the ranks.

If, on his march, he pass villages, farms, or mills, he cannot sufficiently attend to his detachment, even if he should be fully assured that during his march, he has nothing to suspect from the enemy, for in war we ought never to consider ourselves secure. How often have I met with the enemy in a place where I had not the least suspicion of him, and how many parties are cut off during war, owing to the negligence and ignorance of an officer: on the contrary, an officer has

38

nothing to apprehend in the greatest danger, if he have his men fully prepared, and in the best order.

If an officer have reason to suspect that he may fall in with the enemy (on whatever account he may have been sent out by his commander), he cannot be too cautious and circumspect. He ought to appoint a non-commissioned officer and a few privates, in proportion to his force, to march 50 or 100 paces before him; and another small body at the same distance on both sides, whom he must order to keep a good lookout, so that nothing may escape their notice. They must search every covered place on the road. Should there be a wood in the neighbourhood, through which the side flankers are to pass, one or two ought to penetrate quite through it, whilst the others remain at the distance of 100 or 150 paces behind, so that if those in the wood should be carried off by a concealed enemy, the latter can run back to report the occurrence to their officer. If any hill be near, one of them ought to be sent to the top, to observe the country; or when they meet with cultivated fields, one ought to pass through them to be assured that no concealed enemy lie within.

They must conduct every peasant whom they meet to the officer, who ought to question him upon the following points, *viz.* what he knows of the enemy? Where he is? How strong? What kind of troops? Whether he has artillery and baggage? Whether he is watchful and well disciplined, or if his officers ride about the country, and if the men are often marauding and straggling. Should they perceive any danger, one must run back, and make a sign with his hand to the officer, who should immediately go to the place, to see it himself. If he find that he is a match for the enemy's party, and the country favours concealment, he and his men should lie down upon the ground on the side of the road: as soon as the enemy's detachment has passed them, he must fall upon it, and if infantry, with a loud shout, thereby confuse it, and take it prisoner. In case, however, the enemy's party be cavalry, and the country be so intersected, that the enemy cannot charge him, he must wait until they come near, call out to the leader of the detachment. Halt! his men must level, and he must ask them, whether they will lose their lives or alight, and attempt by this means to make them prisoners.

If the enemy be strong, and it be impossible to remain concealed, he should endeavour to observe him, and retire, as soon as he thinks he has remarked everything necessary, to give his commander timely notice of all that he has seen.

If an officer of light infantry has the advance guard, as it may happen in hilly and intersected countries, he may proceed, with respect to the march, in the above-mentioned manner, with this difference only, that he frequently makes a report to his commander of all that he sees; and in this case he will do well, to keep at the head of the advance guard, in order to observe everything himself. In the night time, when the *eclaireurs* and flankers should not advance farther than 20 or 30 paces in front, and cannot see far around them, it behoves him and his men to observe the greatest silence, to lie down often upon the ground, and listen if they can discover anything. It is almost incredible, of what use we may be to our general, if we employ in such instances, suitable circumspection.

On a march by night from Westernover to Richmond in Virginia, where I led the advance guard of Arnold's corps, and when the general could receive no intelligence of the enemy, on account of all the inhabitants of the country having fled from their houses, seven of the enemy (one of whom was a major) fell into my hands at intervals, in the space of two hours: all of them had been sent with written orders from the governor to the different commanders of the militia of the country, which threw a great light upon his operations. Should an officer meet with the enemy unawares in the night, he must give him a volley, and charge with bayonets, without troubling himself farther about his strength, whereby the enemy, as he cannot see the strength of his antagonist, will certainly be puzzled, and the commander will gain time to take proper measures.

If an officer have the command of a lateral *patrole*, he should endeavour to cover that flank of the corps on which he marches, against every possible attack of the enemy. In the daytime he may withdraw 300 paces from the main body, and send a non-commissioned officer with 8 or 10 men to the distance of 150 paces from his flank, which non-commissioned officer may also detach two or three men to the same distance from his flank, who should accurately search the whole country, to see that no party of the enemy be concealed between him and the corps. If there be a hill in the neighbourhood, some should pass over it, to observe the country, and ought not (as I have seen lateral *patroles* do) to remain at the foot of it.

Should they meet with small pieces of water, or morasses, they must not leave them between the corps and themselves, for by this means the lateral *patroles* might be cut off. In general, an officer who is sent with a lateral *patrole*, cannot be too well instructed by his commander, as any carelessness or want of dexterity, may cost many men. For example, the Queen's Rangers and Ferguson's Sharp Shooters on their march in Pennsylvania, some hours before the Battle of Brandywine River on the 16th of September, 1777, fell into an ambuscade, and lost by a well-directed fire of the enemy more than 100 men, owing to the negligence of the lateral *patroles*. The English First Battalion of Light Infantry met with the same missortune, on their march from Pennsylvania to Avington's Hill.

Though an officer may not have discovered anything of the enemy, he ought not however to forget the necessary precaution on his return, for it might be possible, that a party of the enemy had concealed themselves in the neighbourhood, in order to cut him off, or attack him at that time, when officers in general are more liable to conceive themselves secure, and consequently will be less vigilant. For instance, in the campaign of 1780, in the province of New York, I was sent from Philipsburgh to Terretown, to procure intelligence of the enemy, and carry off some of his officers, who were in this place at home, and frequently remained in their houses in the night-time; I left the camp before sunset, and as the road lay up Hudson's River, and its opposite bank was occupied by the Americans, I was perceived by them; a party passed the river in boats in the night-time, in order to attack me upon my return in a *defilé*, which lay half way between our camp and Terretown; but as it began to be daylight, and the enemy found that I returned in the best order, and with every precaution, he did not think proper to attack me, but suffered me to proceed unmolested.

As rules supported by useful examples give the best instruction, I will here mention one from history, which is founded upon the same principle as the above. The Marshal Von Schomberg, who commanded the French army in the Spanish war of 1664, wished to cover Rousillon; he therefore sent off a considerable detachment, to secure the convoy which was coming from Perpignan, and was to pass the village of St. Jean du Page, nine miles from thence; this detachment was posted upon a height near the high road; its commander detached a non-commissioned officer with 30 men, to occupy a chapel a little in front, and which lay 300 paces from the main post, and commanded it, so that the officer could wholly overlook the plain of Boulon, where the Spaniards were encamped; the Spanish parties had to cross the plain in their route, if they intended to make themselves masters of the French convoy: from Boulon to the two posts there was a hollow way, in which the Spaniards could creep, without being perceived; the

Marshal Von Schomberg had therefore occupied another post, near a place called the Red House, in order to secure himself from a surprise, which he might daily expect: this post had orders, as soon as it discovered anything of the enemy, to light a fire, thereby giving notice to the neighbouring posts, and allow them an opportunity of supporting each other in the best manner possible.

A Spanish officer who had the best information, not only of the features of the country, but also of the outposts of the French, had entered the hollow way in the night-time with 40 cavalry, and had placed himself between the three posts, with a design to surprise the officer's detachment, when it should relieve the posts near the chapel, which was generally done in the morning. The French officer had scarcely arrived in the hollow way, when the Spaniards fell upon him unawares, and killed or wounded him and all his men, before he had time to collect himself. The Spanish officer gave the French officer two cuts with his sabre, with this advice: "Learn your duty better for the future, and before you march your men through a country, examine it."

This example shews sufficiently how necessary it is, for every officer to be fully acquainted with the situation of the country, through which he must pass, especially when it is woody and hilly, where he cannot see far before him. Should an officer, however, after having taken every precaution, meet with an enemy unawares, and be attacked on all sides, and can find no resource to return to the place from whence he came, he ought to endeavour to find out a church, mill, or house in the neighbourhood, go to it, occupy it, and rather sacrifice all, than become a prisoner disgracefully. In what manner these posts are best fortified under such circumstances, see the 3rd section of this chapter.

SECTION 2
OF THE DUTY OF AN OFFICER OF LIGHT INFANTRY ON PIQUETS OR OUTPOSTS.

As the rules, to which an officer of light infantry ought to adhere, upon piquet or outposts, very much agree in principle with those which an officer of cavalry ought to observe; I refer the reader, in order to avoid unnecessary repetition, to the first section in the ensuing chapter, and shall only briefly mention the following particulars.

As soon as an officer arrives at his post, has relieved the sentries, and has received every information from the officer whom he relieves, he ought to observe the country with attention, acquaint himself well with the situation of his posts, and enquire where the roads lead; where, and at what distance the enemy is, in order that he may acquaint his superior officers when they visit the posts, with every particular. He must take notice on what side he could retreat, and where and how far he can send his *patroles*. In the daytime, he may allow his men to place their arms together, but is not to suffer them to stroll: as soon as night approaches, he must order one half of his men, either by ranks or platoons, under arms; permitting the other half to rest, but not to sleep by the fire; in which case, they must keep their muskets between their knees, that they may be instantly ready, on the first fire from the sentries.

Should the enemy be near, he must remain with his piquet under-arms throughout the night, and withdraw behind, or on one side of the fire, so that he may not be discovered by him if attacked, and that he may by the help of the fire discover him: it is best, when the enemy is near, to be without any fire, if the weather permit, or at least, to have as little as possible. He ought to send out *patroles* continually, who should visit the chain of sentries; and also between every relief, which in the night ought to take place every hour, send a non-commissioned officer, or trusty private, some hundred paces in front of his sentries, who should lie down upon the ground, and listen if they can hear the enemy. An officer should, especially, be alert and vigilant on his posts, hold himself in readiness for every event that may happen, and adhere strictly to his orders. When the enemy is so near, which often happens with light troops, that the posts on both sides can converse together (for instance, when both armies are separated by a small river) he must not on any account suffer it, and far less fall into that fault himself, for, from this the worst consequences may often ensue.

I once profited by such an opportunity myself, to reconnoitre an American post: it was when Sir Harry Clinton, on his march from Charlestown, wished to pass the Stony River by Stony Ferry, which was occupied on the left bank by Pulawski's corps. On our side, or on the right bank, was a deep morass, across which there was a dyke of 2000 paces in length, extending as far as the very right bank of the river, and which, as the river was not above 200 feet broad, though very deep, could be completely scoured by the enemy with small arms. The English general was informed that a row galley was laying in the river for the defence of this post; several small parties had been already sent out to reconnoitre, but had not been able to approach the bank, on account of the heavy fire of the enemy; I therefore resolved to attempt myself to enter into conversation with the officer; I drew near the post, saw an officer walking on the opposite bank, proceeded on within musket shot, and made a sign with my hat, to make him understand that I wished to speak to him; he consented, and I endeavoured, during our conversation, to discover what I wished, in order to make a satisfactory report to Lord Cornwallis, to whom it was very agreeable information.

SECTION 3
OF FORTIFYING AND DEFENDING CASTLES, CHURCHES, FARMS, AND HOUSES

To fortify and defend such posts, deserves particular attention. A skilful defence frequently contributes to the happy success of great undertakings, and a handful of men is capable, in such case, of resisting a whole army.

A general may indeed assign such posts, but he can contribute nothing to their defence, for this wholly depends upon the skill and bravery of the officers to whom they are intrusted. It requires more sense than experience, and an officer who has theory, will know how to apply it, if he be not flurried by the approach of the enemy, and may on such an occasion acquire uncommon reputation, and establish his fortune.

An officer who may be forced either by necessity to throw himself into such a post, or may be ordered to defend one, ought, in the first place, to take care to turn out the inhabitants. Before he prepare his defences, he should (if time permit) go round it, and observe on which side the enemy may have the greatest advantage, in order that he may there apply the strongest resistance.

Should the post be a church, surrounded by a wall, he ought to occupy both, if he have a sufficient number of men, and make use of the church as a citadel, or in the last extremity, as a place of retreat; for it is always better to oppose more than one obstacle to the enemy.

To this end, the church benches should be placed behind the churchyard wall, that the men may stand upon them, and be enabled to fire over it. The entrance must be stopped up with litter or earth, and before the church door must be dug a wide trench, over which should be laid a plank, in order to go in and out, which must on an attack be withdrawn. Some trees ought to be prepared *en abbatis*, and placed by the church door, which should, as soon as the men who defended the wall have all retreated into the church, be dragged into the doorway; the church benches should be so placed, that the men can fire out of the windows. Before the men who defended the wall retire into the church, it ought to be occupied by a few, in order to favour the retreat of those who defended the churchyard.

If time permit, loop-holes should be made in the church, especially on both sides of the corners, as these are the weakest parts where the enemy may approach without danger, and set fire to it.

If you have a dwelling-house to defend, you may proceed in the same manner; stop up the doors as well as it can be done, and make your defence through the windows, if there has been no time to make loop-holes. The floors of the higher rooms should, however, be taken up a few feet over the doors of every storey, in order to fire down upon the enemy, and be able to drive him back, Should he attempt to occupy the lower room. The roof of the house should be taken off, and the loft covered with litter or earth, that the grenades of the howitzers (if the enemy employ any) may not set fire to it. Stones and clumps of wood should be laid ready in the loft, as also in every room, in order to annoy the enemy if he should storm.

The most resolute men must be stationed on both sides of the entrance, to drive away the most daring of the enemy, who would force their way. Pitchforks should be at hand, to push away the ladder by which the enemy may attempt to mount. Should there be more buildings near the post, which cannot conveniently be occupied, but which, however, might be of great detriment in the hands of the enemy, they ought, if there be time, to be pulled down or burnt; or if through humanity, one does not wish to do so, the side from which the enemy might injure us, should at least be pulled down, or rendered useless. Above all things, the ammunition must, on the attack of the enemy, be sparingly used, and not a shot fired which will not do execution.

Should the enemy send an officer to offer terms, when circumstances require an obstinate resistance, he must not be admitted, but be desired not to approach, as no intercourse will be suffered; or sent back with a surly answer, such as, let him attack boldly, and he will find courageous opponents, or let him come again in a month. By such a resolute answer the enemy may, if he is not absolutely forced to do it, be deterred from an attack. If a skilful officer, after having done everything in his power, finds that the enemy still persists, and becomes so enraged by an obstinate resistance, that there is no hope left of obtaining good terms, he must not, however, be depressed, but encourage his men by his own example to still greater bravery: a brave man will always find resources, when the base and cowardly will shudder; for at such a time, there is no dissembling, and true valour is here distinguished from assumed confidence: greatness of soul, and a real knowledge of war, at no time shine more conspicuous, than in these difficult moments; such qualities give us astonishing and unexpected resources; for what weapon is stronger than necessity, when our welfare and lives depend upon it?

It is scarcely credible, to what a soldier may be brought, by the good example of his officer. By confidence and esteem, he may rouse in him the courage of a lion. How often have I thought that all was lost, and my men panic-struck, when a short and animated speech revived their spirits, and turned the scale. Near Portsmouth in Virginia, I had placed upon a dyke by Scotsbak, a non-commissioned officer with 16 *yägers*; the enemy met and pursued the *patrole*, which I had just sent out, and attacked this post with such fury, that the piquet was forced to give way. I hastened with 16 men to their assistance, and arrived there as the enemy was about to attack it with whole battalions: I ordered the men to stand their ground, the dyke being so narrow, that not more than three men in front could pass at a time: 'here is the spot,' said I, 'where you may, as Hessians, acquire great reputation in the eyes of the English.' All went well; I was wounded; no *yäger* abandoned me, and the enemy gave up his undertaking, after losing many men: a few *yägers* had the honour of maintaining a post, in presence of the English, which General Arnold had given up as lost, and where he had left the *yägers* unsupported, for fear of sacrificing too many men. After the affair, the general out of national pride was inwardly hurt, to think that a handful of Europeans had resisted, and driven back whole battalions of his countrymen.

I repeat it once more, that when all is lost, we must not be depressed, nor ever think of surrendering, but persuade the men, that there will be no hope of quarter, in order to make them desperate. As soon as it is night, collect your party, silently prepare an issue, sally out on the opposite side to which you wish to retreat, and make your way sword in hand through the enemy; this however must be done with the greatest silence, as the enemy, who perhaps by the warmth and fatigue of the day is weary, and quiet, considering his booty as certain, will not expect so bold an attempt; for night is the mother of fear, and astonishing things may be undertaken with its assistance.

The following example will support my assertion, and shew how far an able defence of these kind of posts may contribute to success in the great occurrences of war. Sir William Howe, in the American campaign of 1777, had his camp before German Town, two leagues from Philadelphia, which was supported on the right by the River Delaware, and on the left by the River Shulkil, near the Waterfall. General Washington being acquainted with the lethargy of the English general, had advanced as far as Narrentown, and made a forced march in the night of the 3rd and 4th of October, and attacked at daybreak the right wing of the English army so furiously and unexpectedly, that the light infantry, which was posted half a league in front of this wing, was completely routed.

The then Lieutenant Colonel Musgrave, who was posted near Tew's House with three companies of the 40th regiment of foot, a little distance behind the light infantry, had scarcely time to take up arms; he perceived in a moment, that should he retreat, the army which was in perfect security would have hardly time to take up arms; he therefore immediately resolved to throw himself and the three companies (which did not amount to more than a hundred men) into the above-mentioned house, from which he could command the road the Americans must take; but as the enemy was so close upon him, that he could not make any great preparations for defence, he had the house doors blocked up with tables and chairs. General Washington, who could not turn this post, and was exposed to its galling fire, remained (fortunately for Sir William Howe) with his whole army near this post, which a single regiment might have masked; he had artillery brought up, and ordered his best regiments to attack it: Lieutenant Colonel Musgrave, who preferred the honour of the British nation to his life, repeatedly repulsed the enemy with great slaughter, and held out against a whole army, until Sir William Howe, being roused from his slumber, approached with his army, and drove General Washington back again with a severe loss, for which favourable turn, Sir William Howe had alone to thank the bravery and judgement of Lieutenant Colonel Musgrave and a handful of his valiant countrymen; for had the latter had less presence of mind, and retreated, the right wing, who thought themselves perfectly secure, could not have got under arms in time, and the whole army would undoubtedly have been disgracefully routed (especially as even after the firing of the light infantry had began, the news of the approach of the enemy was rejected at headquarters as false and impossible), having Philadelphia full of rebellious inhabitants, and the Delaware in the rear.

I really believe, that few generals have ever been in a more critical situation, and owe more to fortune, than Sir William Howe on the above-mentioned day. Had the Hessian officer, who was posted with 50 *yägers*, not far from Trainton near the great house, fortunately acted upon the same principle on the approach of Washington, the three regiments would not have had the misfortune to become prisoners, and Colonel Rall (who had always been reckoned a very good and skilful officer) had not here lost his life, nor the reputation which he had acquired in the seven years war.

I do not mention this, with an intention to censure the actions of great men, but merely to shew how necessary it is, that an officer should study his profession in his youth; for from the least carelessness, or the least fault in war, whole provinces, and indeed whole nations may be lost. An officer who takes a pleasure in studying such examples, and is desirous of information, should read the *History of Charles the 12th*, published by Adlerfeld, which is full of truly heroic actions.

SECTION 4

OF THE EXCURSIONS OF SMALL PARTIES OF LIGHT INFANTRY

It is astonishing, that the power of making incursions into the enemy's country with small parties, is ascribed to hussars alone. One cannot easily find an example in the history of the seven years war, of an officer of light infantry having distinguished himself in this manner. In the American war it was the contrary; for the light infantry alone was intrusted with this duty, and we cannot remember any example excepting one, where a small party of cavalry have performed this duty: this was, when Sir William (now General) Harcourt carried off General Lee from his quarters. On the contrary, how many examples can be given during that war, where small detachments of the American light infantry have carried off generals and officers of the English army from the midst of their quarters.

I am therefore fully convinced, that with light infantry as many excursions may be undertaken as with cavalry, especially in intersected countries; for instance, in Holstein and Sleswick, where one may by the help of frequent coppices creep along undiscovered; the light infantry has this advantage over the cavalry, that they can conceal themselves with facility, and the highest hills, the thickest woods, and the most impenetrable, morasses, are no obstacles to them. Moreover, light infantry are not necessitated to provide for horses, and have only to think of their own subsistence. Lakes and navigable rivers are more easily crossed by foot soldiers than cavalry, for at every place which lies upon a river, may be found boats to carry them over, which can be seized in the night-time with very little trouble.

In the American war, who could have checked the excursions of the New Englanders, and the militia of the province of New Jersey, upon Long Island, though the former were separated by the mouth of the River Hudson, and the latter by the Streight from the English possessions; and how few of their parties, each of which only consisted of 8 or 10 men, had the misfortune to be taken prisoners? What distant excursions have not Brand and Butler undertaken? They have gone more than once, with a handful of men, from Canada into Pennsylvania, and I really believe, that if these two enterprising men had been supported by the English, the conclusion of that war would not have been so disadvantageous to Great Britain. But some may say, these were Indians!—but there were also Europeans with them, who, to be sure, were not so effeminate as our *petit-maitres* are, who cannot live an hour without bread and strong liquors. These men often lived whole months upon game, and why cannot Europeans live upon it also? If an officer only take a delight in this kind of warfare, and introduce that severe discipline, that no soldier dare attempt to murmur, he will find nothing too arduous, though it may even appear impossible.

In the campaign of Virginia, the army had frequently no bread, and I never heard them murmur. I had once 10 or 12 *yägers* who were without shoes, and were forced to make shift with cow hides; they began to grumble, I punished one of them severely, and the rest were in a short time so reconciled, that they were joking each other upon their new fashioned kind of shoes. For these enterprises, none but resolute men are fit; men accustomed to a rigid discipline, alert, used to marching, and who, by the hardships of war, are enured to everything, with an officer at their head who understands his profession, knows how to acquire a proper knowledge of the countries through which he must pass, and braves every difficulty which would appear impossible to be surmounted to the common herd of men.

Supposing for instance, an army be in Lower Hessen, Westphalia, or Hanover, and the enemy have occupied Gottingen, Cassel, Marburg, Giesen, Hanau, Frankfort, and all the posts on the Rhine as far as Coblentz; who can hinder an officer with 20 or 30 men from going from Westphalia into the neighbourhood of Rhinefels and Coblentz to levy contributions, and put all the garrisons into such fear, that no one dare any longer trust himself out of the gates; for the farther we are from the theatre of war, the less we hazard; and under such circumstances, many couriers and chief officers must fall into our hands. Supposing all these garrisons, vexed to see their officers carried off in such a manner from their very gates, should exert themselves to destroy or take this detachment, how can they succeed against those who are here today and gone tomorrow; who can so easily conceal themselves behind every bush, and find plenty of retreats, and steal in safety through the large forests, with which Germany is covered.

An officer who wishes to apply himself to this duty, in which he may gain great reputation in the world, should especially acquire a knowledge of those countries through which he must pass. He may be assisted by two means. In the first place, he ought to have good maps, and secondly, should learn by questioning the inhabitants of the country, as to the direction of the roads, the distance of towns, where there are forests, hills, hollow ways, *defilés*, ferries, and bridges, all of which he ought to compare with his map.

When you leave any place, it should be done as secretly as possible, march in the night-time, and during the day lie concealed in the thickest forests. During the night you should approach the highway between two of the enemy's garrisons, and endeavour to cut off couriers or officers. But every detachment you may find in your way, however weak, must be left unmolested; for in this case you do not go out to fight, but to annoy the enemy without endangering yourself. If you be forced to march in the daytime, endeavour to avoid all inhabited places and highways, that the country people may not betray you, and when you meet with a single inhabitant, whoever he may be, take him along with you, as long as your safety requires, however, to treat him with civility, and not suffer the men to insult him, as a contrary behaviour would exasperate and incite him to revenge, whenever an opportunity offers.

Should want of provisions oblige you to enter a village, approach it by night, remain concealed in the neighbourhood, and send into it a non-commissioned officer with a few men; he should endeavour to learn in the first house where the lord of the manor or the municipal officer resides, demand provisions for several hundred men, take as much as you want, and oblige them to carry it to the place where the detachment is concealed: question the peasants about the roads and places where you have no thoughts of going, permit them to return, and march for some leagues in the direction of the road which you intend to take the next day.

When you wish for information respecting the country or the enemy, you must endeavour to surprise in the night-time some nobleman or officer, priest or forester, in his own house, who may give you the necessary information, of which make memorandums upon your map. If in an enemy's country, give yourself out for an officer of their army. In Virginia, when I gave myself out as an *aid-de-camp* to the Marquis de la Fayette, this deception would in all probability have succeeded, if the appearance of two English marauders had not accidentally betrayed the approach of the English army; as an American municipal officer would have ignorantly been the cause of my carrying off an American colonel.

One may make use of another artifice to procure information: give yourself out as an officer, who leads the advance guard of a strong corps, which is destined upon a secret expedition: for example, in the winter expedition of 1776, when Colonel Donop wished to penetrate as far as the neighbourhood of Philadelphia, I was sent from Bourdentown, in the province of New Jersey, to Burlington, with only 1 officer, 30 grenadiers, and 10 *yägers*, the colonel not wishing to expose more men: this was to get intelligence whether the American row galleys held their stations in the Delaware near that town. I had to pass in my route within two leagues of the right flank of the corps under General Mifflin, who was quartered in and all round Montholly, and whose parties were ranging the country as far as Burlington, in order to maintain a communication with this town, and cover his left flank.

At daybreak, I arrived safely at Yorkshire Bridge, a short half league, from Burlington: I found two houses near the bridge, which I immediately so surrounded, that no one could come out. Fortunately for me, there was so great a fall of snow that nobody was upon the road, and the enemy's parties, owing probably to the bad weather, kept themselves in their quarters. I made every enquiry of the inhabitants of both houses, especially respecting the row galleys. One assured me, that Burlington was occupied by the marines of the galleys, which were at anchor before the town. The other, however, assured me quite the contrary. As I should have been ashamed to return with a false report, I desired one of the inhabitants to conduct me to the mayor of the town, took two *yägers* and two grenadiers with me, leaving the men concealed behind the two houses, and directed my officer, in case he should hear any firing in the town, to consider it as a sign, that the enemy was there, and I taken prisoner: upon which he must make the best of his retreat through the forests up the Delaware, and report the whole affair to Colonel Donop.

I went on direct for the mayor's house, which was at the entrance of the town, remained on horseback, and took my servant with me, who was well armed, having ordered the four men to follow me, at the distance of 100 or 150 paces, directing the first to keep within sight of me. As soon as I fired a pistol, they were to discharge their pieces in the town, and save themselves as well as they could. I arrived at the mayor's house, and called him to the door, who, being no friend to the English, answered all my questions equivocally, and with a mysterious countenance. I commanded him in a surly manner to provide sufficient provisions for Colonel Donop's corps, who were approaching, rode full gallop through the town to the bank of the Delaware, and reconnoitred the row galleys, which were lying at anchor in the middle of the river. A mob soon collected, some of whom appeared to be seamen, and looked upon me with astonishment, as I did not speak a single word to them. I galloped back again through the town, called the four men to me, retreated as fast as I possibly could, and arrived safely at Bourdentown, where they had almost given me up as lost.

I mention this example to shew the young officer, that he must not always fully rely upon the intelligence of country people; and that it is better to fall a sacrifice, than to outlive the shame of having made a false report, which might be productive of the worst consequences. It is scarcely credible, how much that man will hazard, who prefers honour to life, and the general good to his own. The saying of Xenophon cannot be too much attended to:—"*Why do I wait any longer to distinguish myself in the world?*"

SECTION 5
OF PETARDS.

As I have promised in the first section to treat of the use of petards, I think it cannot be better introduced, than in this chapter, in which I am treating of the duty of an officer of light infantry.

The prejudice which many persons of great military knowledge have against using the petard, may arise perhaps from the example of the best generals of the present age, who have never made use of it, and we can only remember one instance, in a long series of years, where it has been used. This was at the siege of Bender in the last war, between: the Russians and Turks, when the former employed one in storming that town, and which Captain Stein attached, and thereby rendered his name immortal. Be as it may, there is however no rule without an exception, and I am fully convinced, that it might be employed on many occasions in war. For instance, why could it not be used to break open the gates of a small town, surrounded with a wall and a shallow ditch, of which there are so many in Germany? Such a place, if defended by enterprising men, sword in hand, may offer great obstacles, and cost many men. But when once a petard is properly fixed against the gates, there will be no great difficulty in opening them by the assistance of a few carpenters with a trifling loss, as they must already be shattered to pieces by its explosion.

It may be said perhaps, that this can be done with artillery. True: but if we wish to carry on speedily a secret and important enterprise, we cannot take much artillery along with us, and perhaps none at all, when on the contrary, a few petards are easily carried; besides, a few cannon balls have but little effect upon gates, make only a hole through without shattering them, especially if they be old and rotten and do not resist the ball; moreover, it requires a great number of shots, and much time to shatter them to pieces, and at the same time spreads an alarm. The petard, however, makes but one explosion, and the gates are shattered at once.

It may also be said, that several brave and skilful officers might probably lose their lives before they could succeed in attaching the petard. I do not mean, that it must be used where the enemy is prepared, but only when we can come unawares upon him, and when there is no time to be lost. It is especially useful to light troops and flying corps, as some of them may be conveyed with less inconvenience than the smallest field piece. Had Colonel Donop been furnished with a few, or indeed with only one petard at the attack of Redbank, this brave man would doubtless have been successful, and many a valiant Hessian grenadier, and many an excellent soldier of Young Lorberg's regiment, would not have fallen a sacrifice; for these resolute men had reached the gates before the Americans were aware of it, but which their courage alone could not open, and thus these uncommonly brave men fell victims, one after another; we had some howitzers and 6 pounders with us, but the situation of the gates prevented our using them. I conversed upon this affair with one of the French officers, who served at that time as a volunteer with the Americans, and who had been in this place during the attack; his opinion corresponded exactly with my own.

As the petard belongs to the science of artillery, which is studied

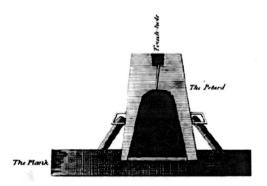

Touch hole

The Petard

The Plank

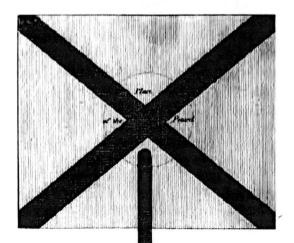

Plan of the Petard

The Hook to fasten or suspend the Petard to a gate

A Foot

1 2 3 4 5 6 7 8 9 10 11 12 *Inches*

by few, (though every officer should endeavour to acquire as much knowledge of each branch of the art of war as is indispensably necessary, in order that when he arrives to a higher rank, and may happen to have the command of a few field pieces, he may not find himself in the dangerous situation of not knowing how to use them) I will here offer a short description of the petard, sufficient to give an officer some idea of it; whereby, should an opportunity occur, he will know how to act. The adjoined plate will give a still clearer idea of it.

Petards are in general delivered ready from the park of artillery; but as I know from experience, that in case of necessity, any large apothecary's or kitchen mortar may answer the purpose, I will explain the art of loading them; and as many officers, though desirous of information, may not, either because they cannot afford, or have no opportunity to purchase books on artillery, I will here cite the instructions of Mr. Le Blond and Mr. Von St. Remy. Respecting the necessity of establishing a military library in every garrison, I will leave to the judgement of military men.

The first says, warm the petard in such a manner, that you can bear to lay your hand upon it. Put into it 2½ inches deep some very fine gunpowder, that has been sprinkled with spirit of wine, and carefully beat it down, so that the powder keeps its grain; over this, put a thin layer of sublimate mercury, then powder, afterwards mercury, and so on, until it is full. Cover the charge with two sheets of paper, lay an inch thick of *etoupille*, and beat all firm together. Pour over it a melted composition of one pound of brick-dust and half a pound of pitch or *calophonium*, which must be covered with an iron plate half an inch thick, having three prongs fixed into a strong piece of plank, observing that the plate fit the petard exactly. Press this plate upon the above composition, when warm, in order that what is superfluous may run over the sides. One may also pour some of the composition round the rim of the plank, and fasten the petard to it before the materials cool. The pipes leading to the touch-hole must; be made of iron, and about 3 inches in length.

The latter says, put into the petard double the quantity of powder it would contain without forcing it down, and cover it with strong double paper or felt, upon which lay wooden plugs of the same size as the bore, which should be knocked down upon the powder, though so carefully, that the powder preserves its grain; then fill up the remaining space of the petard with tow, yellow wax, or Greek pitch, and cover the whole with waxed cloth.

But as the above foreign materials cannot always be at hand when necessity requires, and as the powder alone is the cause of its operations, I will communicate a shorter method of loading it.

Fill up the interior with powder in such a manner, that you have forced into it double the quantity that it would contain without any pressure or shaking, taking care that the powder preserves its grain, as it would otherwise lose much of its power. When it is filled up in this manner within three quarters of an inch of the top, lay tow upon the powder, and over this a wooden plug, which must fit the bore of it exactly. Cover this with a doubled linen cloth, which has been dipped in turpentine, or some essential-oil, and pitch it all over so well, that the air cannot come to the powder. Afterwards fasten the petard with iron hoops and screws upon the piece of plank, drive a tin pipe into the touch-hole, and fill it with one part of saltpetre and two of meal powder mixed together.

The petardeer, who is commonly an officer who volunteers for that service, by which he may acquire the greatest honour, and establish his fortune, takes the petard, a hammer, some strong nails, and a lighted match, approaches the gates as privately as he can, to which he intends to attach it, drives in a nail, hangs the petard upon it, and having sufficiently secured it, sets fire to it, and either lies down upon the ground, or runs off until it has burst: the latter, however, is the more dangerous. As soon as it has inforced its effects, the detachment advances near, with a number of carpenters, who have concealed themselves until such has taken place, hew down the shattered remains, and make themselves masters of it.

One may easily conceive, that such an enterprise will not be undertaken by a man of the lower cast; he must be possessed of the most undaunted courage, and prefer honour to life; for should he be perceived by the enemy, he is sure of being exposed to the most terrible fire, as the enemy will exert his utmost to kill a petardeer. But, however dangerous, very few opportunities will offer, where an officer can better give proof of his courage, and acquire more reputation.

CHAPTER 4

Of the Duty of an Officer of Light Cavalry

SECTION 1
OF GRAND GUARDS.

As the welfare of a light corps or detachment alone depends upon its piquets or Grand Guards, they should be so placed, that their rear be free, in order that the enemy cannot surprise them by the help of a bush, wood, or such like covert. Their *videttes* must be so posted, that they can command an extensive view on all sides, and that nothing can approach unnoticed.

If the country permit, you cannot do better than place the Grand Guard behind the crest of a height, in order to conceal it from the enemy. The officer or non-commissioned officer will do well to choose, during his guard, such a station for himself, as to have his in fight, in order that if one of them fall back full speed, he can hasten to meet him, and learn the cause as soon as possible, and thereby be able to make a timely report of it to his commander.

The *videttes* must be double, and posted in the daytime in open places on some rising ground in the neighbourhood, to the distance of 400 or 500 paces in front of the post. In the night it is best to place them so as to look up hill, for a man on horseback will see further in this manner than if he looked to the plain.

The *videttes* must keep their pistols or carbines in their hands, and be well instructed to look continually around them, that they may not be surprised by the enemy: as soon as they discover anything of him, one of them must give a signal by a shot, and gallop back to make his report to the Grand Guard.

Should the country be so interfered, that the *videttes* cannot see far before them, they should be placed double, within sight of each other, and posted as forward as possible, which should be particularly done near hollow ways, that have many windings which hinder an extensive view.

The officer or non-commissioned officer of a Grand Guard ought to endeavour to acquaint himself with the country around; and to this end, as soon as he comes on the post he is to occupy or relieve, should ride round it with the relief himself, that he may observe whence the enemy may come, and be prepared for every event.

He should also be acquainted with the country in his rear, that he may know, when attacked, where to retreat. If he should not be covered on this side by posts, or have a safe communication, he ought to secure his rear by frequent *patroles*.

If on the relief of a Grand Guard, an officer find anything faulty, with respect to the stationed *videttes*, that one or more are not placed so advantageously as they ought, and would be better or more securely stationed in another place, he must immediately report it.

In order to avoid any misunderstanding in such cases, it is best to report such particulars in writing; and an officer would do well, always to carry with him pen, ink, and paper or cards, to be ready on like occasions. He must not be satisfied with that mode of reasoning which is too frequent in the army, and say that, the Grand Guard must be well placed, having been there so long,—he who first placed it, must answer for it,—if the enemy come, I will do my duty, and I have nothing more to do.

I have often heard such foolish discourse in war: it is the language of carelessness, and beings of this kind will often construe the necessary circumspection of those of a more active and spirited nature, into anxiety and fear.

I know too well from experience, that there are men, who cannot bear to find others of an inferior rank more skilful than themselves, and whose favour may owing to this be easily lost. To this however an officer should pay no attention, but report any faults he may perceive with due respect, and enjoy the satisfaction of having done his duty.

After an officer has attended to these rules, he may in the daytime permit his men to alight, but allow, however, no one to move from his horse, and far less, suffer him to unbridle.

The horses must be tied to stakes or hedges with halters, in order that the men may mount them in an instant, and be ready on the approach of the enemy.

At the hours of feeding, the commander of the piquet must never permit the whole to be fed at once, but divide his Grand Guard into two divisions, one of which must not feed before the other has done. If the enemy be in sight, and very near, one rank must remain on horseback, whilst the other feeds.

If there be no water near for the horses, and you are so far from a village, that the peasants cannot bring it, you must not allow more than two men at a time to lead their horses to water.

When the officer perceives the enemy approaching, he must immediately order his men to mount, and hasten to some place, where he can best observe his motions; if he find him strong, he must send a report to his commander of all that he has seen; he should choose the most trusty and experienced men of his piquet to carry the intelligence, which should be expressed as clearly as possible: he must not only mention that the enemy is approaching, but should acquaint his commander, whether he be cavalry or infantry, or both; how strong he may think him, and whether he has artillery. If an officer has paid attention to the marching of troops, and has practiced his eye in making remarks upon their number at a distance, by particular objects, he must be enabled to give a satisfactory report: for example, infantry are easily distinguished from cavalry, at the greatest distance, by the shining or glittering of their arms. The greater or less quantity of dust will shew whether they are infantry or cavalry, and whether the enemy be marching in columns. In the night-time, if you place your ear upon the ground, you may judge by the noise, though a league distant, even should the enemy march ever so quietly, whether he is moving on with cavalry or artillery.

If the Grand Guard be so near the enemy, that his and your *videttes* are close to each other, and it be probable that the enemy will move from his camp, an officer cannot be too attentive, to report it immediately to his superiors. Under such a circumstance, he must remain continually with his *videttes* in the night-time, that he may see and hear everything himself It is a certain sign that the enemy will leave his camp, when the piquet and campfires give a greater light, or appear more numerous than usual; and one may foresee when the enemy is likely to break up his camp, by the noise of the servants packing up the baggage.

An officer must report all such particulars to his commander, and avoid falling into the error of that officer, who being posted on the bank of a river, suffered the enemy, encamped on the opposite bank, to march off by twilight uninterrupted, without reporting a single word about it; when on the contrary, had he reported the circumstance as he ought, a considerable loss would have been prevented. General Washington would not perhaps have so easily succeeded on the 3rd of January, 1777, in escaping the snares, into which he had fallen, if the officer who was posted over against his camp on Trentown Creek, had paid proper attention the sudden alteration in the enemy's fires, which were at first large, and at once became small. General Washington in this case would not certainly have been able to execute his *coup de main* upon Prince Town, in the rear of Lord Cornwallis's army.

If the enemy approach in the daytime, and the skirmishers come so near that the officer of the Grand Guard be forced to retreat, he must retire in close order, and leave his *videttes*, whom he should have previously instructed, to act as flankers, and to skirmish with the enemy during his retreat. The officer ought to be particularly attentive to the motions of the enemy during the skirmish, and take great care that none of his party steal by in his rear, and cut him off

As soon as night approaches, the officer must mount with his piquet, and allow no dragoon to alight, except on the greatest necessity. If his men murmur, which will sometimes happen, under the pressure of severe hardships, he must not be influenced by it, but punish it, and threaten to shoot those soldiers who complain the loudest: for though a soldier complain of the severity of his officer, when the hardships are greatest, the officer may nevertheless be assured, that the good and brave soldier knows well how to distinguish the good officer from the careless and inactive, and a soldier will be as ready to approve the conduct of a skilful and active officer, when he finds his severity was necessary, as to murmur against excessive hardships.

The officer of a Grand Guard should in the night-time send frequent *patroles* towards the enemy, often visit his *videttes* himself, and order the non-commissioned officer to visit them also, in order that he may be assured of their vigilance. The *videttes* should never remain inactive in the night, but should be alternately riding towards each other, in order that no enemy's party may steal through between them. Every relief must *patrole* round the posts to the distance of 500 paces in front, observing not to return to the Grand Guard the same way they came.

If an officer hear a shot from one of his *videttes*, he must; send to him immediately a non-commissioned officer and two well mounted men, in order that he may immediately learn wherefore the *vidette* has fired. If the *vidette* make a mistake, the officer should reprimand him, but by no means punish him, nor become passionate for the false alarm, for it is always better that a *vidette* should give a false alarm, than announce the approach of the enemy too late.

If the *videttes* after having fired come full gallop, and announce the enemy, the officer must hazard a non-commissioned officer and some dragoons, and send them with the same *videttes* towards that quarter, in order to ascertain whether the enemy be really approaching. This non-commissioner should have instructions, not to retreat direct upon the Grand Guard, should the enemy press close upon him, but incline to the right or left, keeping up a continual fire with pistols or carbines. The officer must likewise retreat firing, if closely pursued by the enemy, towards one of the wings of the corps from which he has been detached, in order not to obstruct its motions: during this, he must send off by a dragoon frequent reports of every circumstance to his commander.

But should the enemy attack or succeed in surprising in the night-time the rear of the corps, from which the Grand Guard has been detached, and the enemy has not observed the necessary precautions against the Grand Guard; in such a case, the officer, if cool and collected, may with 20 or 30 cavalry turn the fate of the day in his favour. He should form his men in close order, and fall upon one of the flanks of the enemy with a loud shout, who, already in disorder by their attack or surprise, and not knowing the strength of the piquet which thus falls upon them unawares, will be panic-struck. In this case, the Grand Guard should be previously ordered to give no quarter. If an officer be fully determined to conquer or die, such a desperate *coup de main* may be a favourable resource, and establish his reputation.

Section 2
Of the Advance Guard.

The officer of the advance guard of a corps or detachment of cavalry, cannot be too cautious during a march. In order to be aware of the enemy in time, he must order a non-commissioned officer with a few dragoons to ride to the distance of some hundred paces in front, and, according to his strength, an adequate number of men to the same distance from both his flanks, who should continually keep on the lookout. Supposing the advance guard to consist of 30 dragoons: a trusty non-commissioned officer with 8 men may serve as an advance guard to the officer, two of these should ride to the distance of 100 or 200 paces in front of the non-commissioned officer, two more on his right, and two on his left hand, to the same distance; the other remaining two with the non-commissioned officer.

The officer must send on his right, 4 dragoons, who should have with them a trusty lance corporal, to the above-mentioned distance, and on his left, 4 more. These flankers must not pass any height in the neighbourhood without riding up, in order to observe the country, and search thoroughly every covered place; for upon them depends entirely the safety of the march. They must never neglect to report what they discover, to the officer, who should immediately forward such intelligence. In this case, that no time may be lost for the conveyance of information, he ought to keep sight of his flankers: he must also order these flankers to question every person whom they meet respecting the enemy, and bring such of them to him, as are interesting in their reports, or who appear suspicious.

If a *defilé* or village must be passed, some dragoons should file through it, keeping at the distance of some hundred paces, or at least, in sight of each other. The officer must form up with his party near the entrance of the *defilé* or village, and not enter it, until he is assured, that no party of the enemy be concealed on the other side. Before you enter a village, enquiry must always be made about the enemy at the nearest houses.

If on your route you find one or more cross-roads branching off, they must be thoroughly searched by the flankers, and the situation of these roads be reported to the commander, in order that he may himself order them to be masked; for in woody and hilly countries one cannot be too cautious, for fear of inadvertently running foul of the enemy.

For instance, Colonel Dundas, who commanded at Gloucester, a short time before the siege of York, was ordered by Lord Cornwallis to go out a foraging as far as he possibly could into the country. I had the advance guard, which consisted of 100 cavalry and 60 *yägers* and rangers. Having heard nothing of the enemy on the march, I suspected that the officer of the advance guard must have been somewhat negligent in his search and enquiry at the plantations; I therefore took a dragoon with me, and rode to a plantation myself, which lay about 1000 paces on the right of the road, but to which the enemy might have come undiscovered through the woods. As the Duke of Lauzun was with his legion only 17 or 18 miles from Gloucester, I expected to hear something of his *patroles*: I desired the officer during this time to ride gently; but I had no sooner arrived at the plantation, and called out the owner, (who was a very disaffected man towards our cause) than I discovered five or six French hussars, who were separated from me by a hedge, and fortunately for me did not know the environs of the house as well as myself.

I galloped back, and reported this occurrence to Colonel Dundas, who immediately halted, and did not think proper to forage any farther. We had hardly make up our trusses, when the duke appeared with a strong detachment of Virginian militia; there began a sharp skirmish, and we found no little difficulty in making good our retreat. Had I not suspected the officer's negligence in time, and ridden to the plantation myself, Colonel Dundas would have proceeded farther, and as the enemy was far superior in number, we must have been routed, and the probable consequence would have been, that the duke would have entered Gloucester pell-mell with us, or the greatest part of our cavalry have fallen into his hands.

When the officer of the advance guard has discovered the enemy, and made his report in consequence, he must, as soon as the enemy draws near, begin to skirmish with him, and may in this case, if he be assured of support, send his whole party *en tirailleur*, and endeavour to check his progress, to discover his strength, and cover the advancing reinforcement until farther orders.

In the night-time the officer of the advance guard must listen attentively himself, as his flankers cannot at that time advance to a great distance, and should he meet with the enemy, there is no other resource, than to fall upon him. resolutely, in order to embarrass him, and give time to the main body to advance or retreat.

Section 3
Of Lateral Patroles

Having already mentioned general rules for lateral *patroles* in the preceding chapter, I will here only take notice of some few particulars; general rules for *patroles* of cavalry and light infantry being the same.

An officer of light cavalry, when detached to cover either flank of a light corps on the march, must use his utmost diligence, and every possible circumspection, that the enemy do not fall upon the corps unawares.

In this case, the officer will do best to divide his detachment into three parties, keeping one with him in close order, to be ready to charge the enemy should he approach. He should send another party with a non-commissioned officer to the distance of some hundred paces in front of him, which should spread out by parties of twos, search every covered place, and report to the officer whatever they may observe of the enemy. The third party he must send back with a non-commissioned officer to the distance of some hundred paces towards that flank which he is to cover: these must also march two and two slowly and across through every covered place, and gallop to every neighbouring height, in order to look round. Should these discover the enemy, they must fire, and if he be advancing in considerable force, they must not retreat to the corps or detachment, but to the advance or rearguard, by which means the enemy may be deceived, and give an opportunity to the commander of the corps to take him in flank and defeat him.

Thus the lateral *patroles* covering the space of a quarter of a league, the corps cannot be taken unawares.

SECTION 4
HOW AN OFFICER OF CAVALRY OUGHT TO ACT ON A PATROLE.

As cavalry cannot conceal themselves so readily as light infantry, the officer must be the more careful in accomplishing this commission.

Having taken the necessary precautions, which have been already mentioned in advancing, and if the object be to reconnoitre, whether the enemy still remain on the same post, or have occupied any particular post or pass, the officer must advance with the greatest circumspection, and rather too slow than too quick. He must endeavour in approaching to conceal his strength from the enemy. In such a case he will do well, if it be daytime, to form a single rank, and divide it into two parties, at a certain distance from each other, and he himself should ride with some of his best mounted men to reconnoitre well, and accomplish his orders; having succeeded, he must return as quick as possible.

If this duty must be performed in the night-time, he has certainly this advantage on his side, that the enemy cannot discover him at a distance; but he must also be so much the more careful against ambuscades, and double his precautions, when he comes into the neighbourhood of the enemy. He must order his party to halt at the distance of 600 or 800 paces from the enemy's post, and send a trusty non-commissioned officer with one or two well mounted dragoons towards the sentries, who, as soon as they are challenged and fired upon by the enemy, must retire silently: should the enemy have abandoned their post, the non-commissioned officer must halt on the spot, and send back a dragoon to report the circumstance; upon which the officer should advance and ascertain the fact himself. Should the post be near a village, he should enquire from the inhabitants whether the enemy have marched off, and where. He should take back with him such of the inhabitants as have given the most satisfactory answers, in order to serve as guides, should it be necessary to pursue the enemy; he must however previously send off one of his best mounted dragoons to report the retreat of the enemy to headquarters.

For example, in the spring of 1777, when General Washington collected his army near Morristown, in the province of New Jersey, I was sent out by Lord Cornwallis to see whether the enemy had occupied the *defilé* of Boundbruck, for which purpose an officer with 20 dragoons of the 16th regiment was given me. As I had to pass a *defilé* on my march, I took a trusty non-commissioned officer with 10 *yägers* to me, which, in order to cover my retreat, I left at the *defilé*: I knew this country extremely well, having been there with the outpost since the 4th of January, and had skirmished with the enemy between this post and Boundbruck; I arrived behind the plantation by a round-about road, where the enemy had occupied a night-post the whole winter, I found the enemy had left this country, and advanced within half a league of Boundbruck; as I had yet another plantation to pass, which belonged to a violent rebel, I sent two dragoons to fetch him; I had hardly spoken to him, than I received a fire in front, from about 20 or 30 Americans who were in the orchard of this plantation; I galloped back instantly, and had to go through another volley from as many more, who had cut off my retreat; but favoured by an uncommonly dark night, I reached the *defilé* without losing a man, and without any other misfortune but a fall from my horse, and being trodden upon by the English dragoons, by which my leg was severely hurt.

This example shews, that I had not observed the necessary precaution, and had thought myself too secure, because I did not find the enemy's night piquet, and therefore concluded that the enemy had marched off. I Should have done better, had I ordered the owner of the plantation to have been brought to me when at a greater distance; in this case, I should not have hazarded some 20 men, which might have been lost, had not good luck extricated us.

If a patrolling officer find that the enemy be marching with a strong corps, or with his whole force, he must endeavour to conceal himself, so that he may observe the approach of the enemy, but in which task, he must be particularly careful to avoid being cut off; as soon as he is assured of the enemy's approach, he should send two of his best mounted men, in order that should one meet with a misfortune on the road, the other may escape, and convey the intelligence to the commander. If the enemy halt on his march, the officer must do the same at a proper distance; for it may be possible that the enemy have advanced merely to cover a large foraging; if the officer ascertain this, he must immediately acquaint his commander with it.

But should the officer in this case, notwithstanding every precaution, meet with the enemy unawares in an intersected country, as it may happen in woody countries in a cross road, he must endeavour to force his way through; a few men may escape and report the circumstance. I have seen two instances of this kind during the American war, both of which daring attempts succeeded. One was in the campaign of 1777, in Pennsylvania, where a French officer with 20 or 30 American dragoons on their march, in the country of Swedensfurth, forced through between the advance guard and the English army, and though exposed to the heavy fire of some hundred men from the advance guard and the lateral *patroles*, he however lost nothing more than his hat.

The other was in the campaign of 1781, in Virginia, when a noncommissioned officer and six dragoons of Armand's corps, not far from Discant Bridge, forced through between a piquet of the Queen's Rangers and a corps that were just then encamping. One may see by both these examples, that fortune always favours bravery, and frequently rashness.

When intelligence of the enemy is wanted, an officer is sometimes sent out to make prisoners; in this case, he must have recourse either to force or artifice, and should he meet no party of the enemy on his route whom he can decoy by a false retreat, he must endeavour to approach as near as possible to the enemy's *videttes* or sentries undiscovered, gallop with some dragoons upon them, and try to carry one off. Whether he succeed or not, his retreat must be quick.

The French colonel Armand, who commanded a light corps in the American army, succeeded in such an enterprise, near Courland's house, in the province of New York. He galloped about noon upon a piquet of Hessian and Anspach's *yäger* corps, made two prisoners, and though immediately pursued, came away without loss.

The French major Norman succeeded in an attempt of this kind, against a piquet of the English light infantry near Portsmouth, in Virginia, where he galloped at mid-day upon the sentries, and without firing a shot, made the greatest part of the piquet prisoners.

These enterprises are often more successful in the daytime, especially in the middle of summer about noon, as the men are then tired by watching the whole night, and generally think that less vigilance is required, and are consequently more negligent; they may be also attempted with success in the night-time. Some resolute dragoons may be ordered to approach the enemy's sentries, and if discovered, must give themselves out for deserters, and carry off the sentries, if they be credulous enough to believe them. If this should succeed without the enemy's piquet having perceived it, one may ride confidently to the piquet, fall abruptly upon them, cut them to pieces, or make them prisoners.

If an officer on his *patrole* meet with an enemy's detachment, I advise him by all means to proceed cautiously, and not to follow them, as they have been most probably sent out to decoy him into an ambuscade.

Section 5
Of the Duty of an Officer of Light Cavalry on Rear Guard.

The officer of a rear guard must endeavour to keep his men in as high spirits as possible, to guard them against any sudden fear, in case of emergencies; for the flight of a rear guard upon the main body must create confusion, and as the main body can easily support him, the danger can never be very great. If the enemy follow him, he will do best to divide his party into two divisions, one of which he forms in close order, and employs the other to skirmish; these must always remain two and two for mutual support, and must follow (keeping up a continual fire of pistols or carbines) at the distance of 100 or 150 paces, or even 300, according as they are more or less pressed upon by the enemy's flankers. Flankers must always have the pistol in the hand, and the sabre hanging on the wrist.

If the enemy pursue slowly, the firing must be also slow; if the piquet be closely pressed, the fire of the flankers must be the brisker; by this, the commander will be able to judge and act accordingly.

Should a number of flankers of the enemy be too daring, and hazard too far, the officer must charge them, and that expeditiously, for fear of being cut off: I had once myself a narrow escape of this kind,

I had the rear guard of the *yägers* corps on the retreat through the Jerseys in the campaign of 1778, when the English army were retiring from Allentown: my rear guard consisted of 100 men, about 30 *yägers*, and 20 mounted riflemen, under the command of the brave Lieutenant Mertz, in whom I had the greatest confidence. I posted him with some *yägers* behind the huts of the camp, which the English light infantry had occupied, in order to decoy some of the enemy's *tirailleurs* into an ambuscade. Count Pulawsky commanded the advance guard of Washington's army, a man who had great military knowledge, and truly brave, but whom however I was particularly anxious to ensnare, These huts stood in a small plain of 800 or 1000 paces square, surrounded with gently rising heights covered with wood.

The Virginian riflemen, who are very daring, appeared first, and as these men are very poor and eager for booty, I expected they would be tempted to search the abandoned huts; but I was deceived, for they were too cunning, and remained on the summit of the woody height, until Pulawsky appeared on a sudden with his cavalry. Colonel Wurmb, who commanded the whole rear of the army, and who disapproved of my long stay in the valley, sent orders for me to retire instantly, the whole army being too far off already; I obeyed, Pulawsky was astonished at the men who made their appearance from behind the huts; fortunately for me, the enemy lost the favourable moment of taking some 50 men with the greatest ease, whilst I was passing a *defilé* in my rear, which I found on my march out of the plain, and which *defilé* I was unacquainted with, as indeed with the whole country. I had some difficulty in attaining it, and the enemy, after having received some few well-aimed shots from the riflemen, gave up the pursuit.

This shews that an officer who is with the rear, should not be too rash, as any little advantage which he may obtain over the enemy in such circumstances, is likely to animate him to hazard more, and the smallest disadvantage he may afterwards experience, may discourage the main body on his retreat.

CHAPTER 5

Of the Duty of a Light Corps

SECTION 1.
OF THE DUTY OF A LIGHT CORPS WHEN MARCHING AGAINST THE ENEMY.

I will now take notice of the duty of a light corps in the field, and point out how it must be led against the enemy under every circumstance, A commander who has raised and disciplined his corps by the foregoing rules, can proceed with confidence. He can depend upon the courage and fidelity of his men, if he have placed at their head, officers who unite zeal, patience, and bravery with good conduct.

The march of a light corps has various destinations. It may be sent out to occupy a post expeditiously; to cover a certain tract against the enemy; to establish the communication of two armies, or secure convoys against the inroads of the enemy; to carry off those of the enemy, or to annoy him in the execution of his plans; to fall upon his flanks, and endeavour to retard his march; to trace the detachments of the enemy, who have been sent out for the same purpose; to fall upon and disperse them; to lay ambuscades to decoy an enemy's corps, or to raise contributions and take hostages.

The performance of these different duties will lead to enterprises of the greatest importance, subject to many difficulties, and of which the success requires much artifice, resolution, presence of mind, and an accurate knowledge of the country. We should weigh in our minds every event that may probably happen, and by great reflexion, obtain a thorough judgement and skill in this part of the art of war, which will enable us to discover the best possible means of deceiving the enemy.

One cannot accurately lay down all the rules for the various objects that may happen upon a march, for circumstances may occur, which were perhaps never before observed in any war.

The commander of a corps of this description may, if he possess the ability and skill which are necessary to the success of these undertakings, acquire a never-fading reputation: but on the contrary, when he thinks he has done everything in his power, should he for a moment lose sight of the necessary precaution, by being too much elated with past success, he may lose at once his reputation, and the confidence of the commanding general forever.

There is no profession more thankless than that of a partisan, however well this word may found in the ear of a young officer; for though an officer may have served as such during ten campaigns with the greatest *éclat*, and should be unfortunate in the eleventh, his hard-earned same is at once blasted and forgotten. For instance, Colonel Rall, who by his skill and acknowledged bravery had in the seven years war gained the confidence of several generals of the allied army, lost by one act of negligence, his reputation and his life at Trenton, and that merely owing to his contempt of the enemy.

In this kind of warfare, secrecy is the greatest virtue, and never more than two in the corps, whose judgment, presence of mind, information, and courage may be depended upon, should be acquainted with the object of the undertaking. But, however necessary secrecy may be, one at least must be intrusted with the object of the expedition, for otherwise , should the commanding officer be severely wounded or killed, the design would of course be at an end.

As everyone has not an opportunity of travelling, they must be content with the information they can acquire by maps, and by questioning the inhabitants respecting the situation of the country which may be the seat of war. In order to obtain this, they should endeavour to procure good guides for their march; and if so fortunate in their choice as to meet with those who are well acquainted with the country, but cannot be trusted, non-commissioned officers should be ordered to accompany them as a guard; but such guides must be treated in a friendly manner, liberally entertained, and if poor, well paid, particularly when dismissed. By giving these men a glass of wine, a good meal, and a little money, you may acquire the good name and confidence of a whole district.

I have often been necessitated in the American war to seize upon guides by force; for there was not a single person to be found in the whole country, well disposed to the British army; but a good word, liberal treatment, and a few dollars, often caused the most disaffected man to become my friend, and in the end highly valuable: by such treatment you may rely upon it, that in every country there are men who will assist, and seldom betray you.

The greatest security of a light corps upon a march depends upon the precaution and order, with which it is led. The commander must, above all things, observe that every officer rides before his platoon, which should march in the greatest order, and should suffer no one except upon very pressing emergencies to fall out of the ranks. If this cannot be avoided, a non-commissioned officer must remain to see him back to his platoon. But the men should be accustomed to this, when first formed or in peaceable times, for nothing has a more awkward appearance than to see officers when changing quarters, or when marching to manoeuvre, riding in parties in front and rear of the regiment, and the divisions intermixed. If the men are accustomed to this in time of peace, they would not even think of doing otherwise in war.

How did the Prussians gain their advantage over a superior force? By their good discipline, order, and skill in manoeuvring, to which they were accustomed during peace; the Battle of Zorndorf is an evident proof of this, in which the Prussians, during the hottest of the action, preserved a certain order, whilst the Russians fought *sans ensemble*.

Upon a secret expedition, all servants and valets of the army ought to be placed under the command of an officer, and their place assigned upon the march between the corps and the rear guard; for as they commonly ride about, to search for provisions for themselves and their matters, one of them may be taken by the enemy, and betray the approach of the corps. The greatest irregularities frequently happen in villages, owing to this class of men, by which the corps are detested by the inhabitants, and the whole blame falls upon the commander.

As soon as we suspect the least danger from the enemy, an advance guard of 20 or 30 cavalry should be formed, besides a lateral *patrole* of the same force on each flank; their skirmishers must search the country around for a quarter of a league, in order to receive timely intelligence of everything that may approach: I have mentioned above, how an officer must act in these circumstances.

The advance guard of cavalry must be followed by an officer, with the same number of riflemen, in order to support him; these on the enemy's approach must extend two or three together, and endeavour to do execution upon the enemy's flankers, through the intervals of their own, who, if pressed too hard upon and forced to give way, the *yägers* must lay hold of their stirrups, and by this means secure their retreat. If *yägers* be once practiced to this manoeuvre, it would seldom happen, that any would be lost; for light infantry that cannot fight mixed with cavalry is of little use. Hussars, or, any other light cavalry, if they knew what advantage they may derive from such assistance, would exert themselves to favour their retreat.

We must not pursue, however, the method which a certain M——did upon a manoeuvre, who instead of placing a *yäger's* company behind the advance guard, placed it behind the whole column of cavalry, as he could not conceive how the *yägers* could extricate themselves through the cavalry that was behind him, without being trodden under foot by the horses.

If the country be open on the march, the cavalry must follow the advance guard of those riflemen, which are followed by the two companies of riflemen and light infantry; an officer having 10 cavalry, brings up the rear guard, whose duty it is to observe, that neither soldier or servant remain behind.

Cross roads must be masked by a platoon of riflemen or light infantry, who there form up until the rear guard has passed, or that they are successively relieved by the following divisions.

The commander of a light corps cannot be too strict in his orders to the officers or non-commissioned officers, who lead the advance guard and lateral *patroles*, that they direct their flankers to extend as far as possible (though not out of sight of each other) in front and on the side where the enemy is expected: to question and stop all people whom they meet, and send them to the commander of the corps, in order that they may not fall into a snare, which might cost many men, and occasion very serious consequences. If the American officer on the day of the Battle of Brandywine River had been supported in his ambuscade by some hundred cavalry, these, by a charge upon the head of General Knyphausen's column, when the British Rangers were already in confusion, might have done such execution, as to have frustrated the whole plan of General Howe, or at least, by such a momentary advantage have animated the Americans to a more obstinate resistance.

If there be on the march a hollow way, or a river, over which there is a bridge to be passed, the detachment of riflemen that belong to the advance guard, must file on both sides of the bridge or *defilé*, and occupy the banks of the former, or the heights of the latter. The advance guard of cavalry may then pass, and must search the country far in front, and on both sides for half a league, in order to obtain information of the enemy from the neighbouring inhabitants, during which time the corps form up on both sides of the issue of the *defilé* or bridge. The officer of the advance guard takes post as soon as he has ordered his flankers to search the country about one-eighth of a league distant from the issue of the *defilé* or bridge, reports to the commander of the corps what may occur, and proceeds upon his march in the before-mentioned order.

By this means, intelligence of the enemy may be easily acquired, should any of his detachments be situated in the neighbourhood of the post, and obtain sufficient time to resolve, whether to attack the enemy, maintain the post, or retire.

If an enemy's detachment have occupied such a post, and there are orders to take it by force, or to fight the enemy wherever found; no time should be lost, especially if it be a *defilé*, to charge the enemy resolutely with the light infantry, during which, both the rifle companies must endeavour to take the enemy in flank, and if possible, in the rear.

If the post be a stone bridge, which the enemy have not been able to demolish, the riflemen must endeavour to amuse him along the banks of the river, whilst the cavalry attempt to pass over or under the bridge, and if the enemy cannot hinder it, he must retire. In both these instances, the cavalry must be sent after him, the light infantry follow, and try as much as possible to annoy him upon the road.

For example; General Arnold on his march from Smithstown to Portsmouth in Virginia, perceived that the enemy had occupied the bridge near M'Key's Mill, which lay on the right bank of the River Payan, with some hundred sharpshooters and a field piece, in order to secure this pass, or at least to force General Arnold to take a great round through a country where there were no roads. Colonel Simcoe was sent off with his cavalry to reconnoitre this post. He was hardly on the road, before he sent back an officer to the general with the intelligence that the enemy intended to defend it.

General Arnold ordered me to hasten there with 50 riflemen and 3 companies of rangers with all possible speed. We arrived in the afternoon on this side of the River Payan, and found that the enemy had occupied not only the mill, but the garden, which lay upon a hill on the right. As there was a plantation on this side of the mill, near which stood an orchard, I occupied the latter with my party, and directed a well-aimed fire upon those of the enemy who held the garden near the mill. During this time Colonel Simcoe attempted to ford the river a short half league below the mill. The enemy perceiving this, quitted the post; I pursued him immediately with the *yägers* and a ranger's company over the ruins of the bridge; upon which Colonel Simcoe hastened on the Suffolk road towards me, and the enemy's detachment was almost destroyed. If the *defilé* be so situated, that one cannot go round it, or the bridge be of stone, which the enemy cannot demolish, and he have occupied the *defilé* or both banks of the river, divide the sharpshooters (if you be forced to attack the enemy) into two parties, and order them to keep up a continual fire upon him from both sides of the *defilé* or the bridge; you may also, in case of necessity, order the mounted riflemen to alight, whilst you attack the bridge with the light infantry.

In case of success, and the enemy be driven back, the cavalry must follow immediately, in order to hinder him from making head again. If the enemy by this means should be overcome, the favourable moment must be well employed, and press on him so closely, that he will not hazard another attack for some time.

Should the march be through hilly countries, the sharpshooters should occupy the hills on both sides, in order to cover the corps. Every company must in this case be divided into 8 or 10 sections, all of whom must have their flankers, that they may cover and search a greater tract. These should have good guides to direct them through the footpaths, which lead out of the main road, in order that they may be searched to the distance of a quarter of a league, so that no party of the enemy may steal by, and fall upon the corps unawares in the flank or in the rear.

If the roads in the hills be so narrow that you cannot march by platoons or sections, and are forced to file to the right or left, the heights must be so much the more strongly occupied, in order to march with safety. In this case, the advance and rear guards must consist of light infantry, and the cavalry follow behind both companies of light infantry; a trusty non-commissioned officer with some light dragoons may however be sent with the advance and rear guards, who, should anything happen, will be ready to report the circumstance immediately to the commander.

If the country be woody, the riflemen must cover the advance and rear guards and both flanks, divide into sections, as in hilly countries, and search the coverts a quarter of a league straight forwards, as well as on both sides. These sections, upon which the safety of the corps depends, must not remain behind each other in countries where they cannot see far around them, but must out-wing each other towards the enemy.

By this means a company can search a district of half a league wide, and if attacked, one section covers the other. In the same manner, the two light infantry companies must march into the wood on both sides, and the cavalry proceed between them upon the road.

When marching in the night, which is the best time for secret expeditions, it is well to double the advance guard, in order that they may fall upon the enemy with more effect, for flankers cannot go far out in the night-time to look around. To judge how an officer should act in this case, I refer the reader to the foregoing sections.

Should an officer stumble upon the enemy with his advance guard, he must form up with the whole immediately, on both sides the road; if in a plain, the cavalry should be placed upon the flanks of the light infantry, and the riflemen drawn up behind the cavalry; for as the enemy in such an occurrence will be equally embarrassed, there will be nothing to fear. In this case, some scouts of two or three men may be sent towards the enemy, who, creeping upon their hands and knees, approach his front and flanks unobserved, and thereby form an idea of his strength: from their report and his instructions, the officer will be able to judge whether he must wait until daybreak, or retreat.

An officer may also be sent out to procure intelligence of the approach of the enemy, in which case, as it generally takes place in the night, I would recommend him to proceed still more cautiously, for it may happen, that he will find him where he least expelled him. For example. In the year 1781, when the French and American army had encamped upon the heights of White Plain, and had advanced their outposts as far as Top's Ferry; on the 21st of July, General Clinton having an intention to forage the whole country between the Sawmill and Hudson's River as far as Philip's and Valentine's Heights, in order to be beforehand with the enemy who was approaching, ordered on the evening of the 22nd, Lieutenant Colonel Emmrich to go with a detachment up Hudson's River, and occupy the heights of Top's Ferry; but after midnight, when 2000 waggons with the necessary escort had already arrived upon York Island near the King's Bridge, the general received intelligence that the enemy's army was in motion, upon which he recalled the foragers.

Lieutenant Colonel Pruschenk was instantly ordered with 200

yägers and 30 light dragoons to gain the pass of Philip's Bridge, in order to favour the retreat of Lieutenant Colonel Emmrich, and to cover and support his rear and right flank, should he be attacked. General Washington, who had received the preceding day certain intelligence that De Lancy's volunteers were to go a plundering on the next day as usual, sent the same night a detachment of his best troops about Miles's Square, to form an ambuscade behind the heights that lay between King's Bridge and Morisine, where De Lancy's corps were quartered, in order to attack and defeat them upon their march; of all which General Clinton had not received the least intelligence. Lieutenant Colonel Pruschenk had hardly marched a quarter of a league when his flankers, who were fortunately commanded by an excellent officer (Lieutenant Schaffer), discovered some concealed sentries of the enemy: the non-commissioned officer of the party, a man of extraordinary presence of mind, and of great courage, supposing them to belong to De Lancy's corps, wished them "Good morning;" but as they attempted to seize him, he perceived his error, and cried aloud, "Rebels are here!" extricated himself from their hands, and fired.

Lieutenant Schaffer, who had already advanced farther with the advance guard upon the road of Courtland's plantation, but who marched with every precaution, was likewise informed by his flankers, that they thought they saw some men before them. The officer had hardly called out to them to look attentively before them, as the day was breaking, than they received a fire from the enemy, by which the greater part of them were either killed or wounded. He returned the fire, but finding himself surrounded by the enemy on all sides, resolved to cross a morass which was upon the right, and by which he fortunately escaped.

Lieutenant Colonel Pruschenk, who was meanwhile endeavouring to gain a height, formed up, attacked the enemy resolutely, and routed him after a treble attack. Colonel Wurmb hastened to his assistance with the remaining part of the Hessian *yäger's* corps; the enemy was driven back beyond Devan's plantation, and the detachment under Lieutenant Colonel Emmrich saved. The enemy left upon the field more killed and severely wounded than the whole of the *yäger* detachment, whose loss amounted only to 37 killed and wounded.

Should you be sent out to cover the rear of another detachment, or to support it, every means ought to be employed to accomplish the object: the preceding example is worthy of imitation, which also proves, that you should never think yourself fully secure; for had this detachment been surprised and cut off, it would not only have been lost, but also that under Lieutenant Colonel Emmrich, whose fortunate escape depended upon it; and the loss of those detachments would have been irreparable to so small an army as General Clinton's at that time was.

Colonel Pruschenk here acted in the best manner possible; for, had he lost his presence of mind, and delayed, Lieutenant Colonel Emmrich, who was already pressed upon by the enemy, would have been lost. There are circumstances in war, when all must be hazarded, and at one time measures may be undertaken with propriety, which at another would be rashness and foolhardiness.

As often as you halt or encamp upon a secret expedition, you ought to avoid inhabited places, and choose the most covered countries; observing however, that you have water in the neighbourhood. If the bread which you had brought with you be finished, send a trusty non-commissioned officer, after you have fully examined that you be in safety, with chosen men to the nearest village, in order to raise what you may want. Under such circumstances, order this party to bring back with them the lord of the manor, a municipal officer, a priest or forester, to procure intelligence from them. If you be in an enemy's country, you may keep any of them with you as long as convenient, signifying to the inhabitants, that should you discover any treachery, these hostages will be hanged.

If you find that an enemy's detachment occupy the neighbourhood whence necessity compels you to fetch provisions, and you cannot attack him owing to his superiority, or for other reasons, you must not remain a moment longer than you have received the necessary provisions, but march a few leagues to one side, or even to the rear, and turn again by a round-about way to the road which you are to follow, in order that the inhabitants may not betray you, who in general cannot spare much, and therefore will not give willingly. It is best to pay ready money for the bread, when you are in critical circumstances, and only take as much as necessity requires.

If sent out to seize an important post, to take hostages, or to lay in ambuscade for an enemy's convoy, you must avoid an engagement, even if certain of success, for fear of losing your principal object, and acting contrary to your orders. If you be however forced to engage with an enemy's detachment upon your march, you must not be too long in resolving, make your disposition immediately, and charge him resolutely, though superior; for it is a general rule in war, that he who begins the attack, has already half the victory, and fortune generally favours the resolute and brave, and very often indeed the rash. In case the country be flat, fall upon one of the flanks of the enemy with the greater part of your cavalry and light infantry, whilst the riflemen, supported by the other part of the cavalry, will amuse the other wing of the enemy by a false attack: the riflemen must endeavour by their destructive fire to annoy and weaken the enemy on all sides from afar; for should once one of the enemy's wings be thrown into confusion, and begin to waver, the other wing will soon follow the example, and a general route be the consequence. In case the country be intersected with woods or hills, you must fall upon the enemy on all sides by platoons or divisions, and you may employ your riflemen to great advantage in such countries, where the cavalry or bayonet can be of little or no effect.

On an attack, divide your corps into two parts, and send them upon both wings of the enemy. The advance guard of the corps under the Marquis de la Fayette was defeated in this manner near Spencer's House, not far from Williamsburg. In the campaign in Virginia, the army under Lord Cornwallis quitted their camp near Psaun's Plantation on the 25th of June at sunset, and directed their march towards Williamsburg. Colonel Simcoe was to cover the left flank of the English army, with his corps and the *yäger* detachment, to take his march between the rivers Chikahomming and Discant, to carry off the cattle, destroy the boats he might find in both rivers, and to burn the tobacco manufactories. Hereupon he divided his corps into two divisions, with one of which he marched himself along the left bank of the Chikahomming, and I remained with the other upon the right bank of the Discant. We were informed upon the first and second march by some well disposed people, that the enemy was pursuing us: we were indeed upon our guard; but being generally not farther from our army than four or fix leagues, we laughed at this intelligence, and considered it as some contrivance they had in view to send us out of the neighbourhood as soon as possible.

Without attending to this, we determined to adhere strictly to our orders, more especially as on the 25th we received intelligence near Burben's Plantation, that Lieutenant Colonel Tarleton had halted the same day near Pund's Plantation, a league and a half on my right, with the British legion, who formed the rear of the army.

I hastened to Colonel Simcoe over Soan's Bridge, where the Discant falls into the Chikahomming; we came through the passes of

Narwells and both Coopers' Mills, and arrived safe on the 26th, at seven o'clock in the morning, at Spencer's Plantation, two leagues from Williamsburg, where the army then was, bringing with us 1200 head of horned cattle.

As we had marched the whole night, the colonel ordered us to rest ourselves a few hours in the wood on the sides of the road. The cattle was driven under a small escort before us, and as we thought ourselves in perfect safety, only a few sentries were placed. I had the advanced guard with the *yägers*, one company of grenadiers, and one of light infantry; the battalion of Rangers followed, after these the cattle, then the cavalry, and a Scotch company with the colonel brought up the rear.

The country was interfered with wood, morasses, and heights. The cavalry was sent to water by platoons, at a rivulet which wound through a valley on the left, and was not far from the place which the Scotch company had occupied.

The enemy, to whom all the inhabitants were well disposed, and who on the contrary hated us, because we had done them much injury in the execution of our orders as to the disaffected subjects, was arrived so near us by a very quick march, (without our having received any intelligence of it), that we had hardly time when the sentries gave fire, to take up arms.

Fortunately for us, the American Major Macphersn, who fell upon a part of the cavalry whilst watering their horses, attacked somewhat too soon, and thereby gave the alarm. I sprang upon my horse at the first shots, and hastened through an orchard that was straight before me, in order to look round; I perceived, at the distance of a gunshot, a line of infantry, a part of which inclined to the left, in order to cut us off from Williamsburg's road: I galloped back again; a French officer pursued me, but was taken prisoner by my orderly dragoon: I cried out, "forward!" ordered the *yägers* to incline to the right, that they might fall upon the flanks of the enemy, if it were possible, or at least to maintain the road to Williamsburg, and charged the enemy with the companies of grenadiers and light infantry without firing.

The Scotch captain, M'Key, did the same on the enemy's right; and Captain Schenk, with the few dragoons and hussars which he had collected together in haste, fell upon the enemy's cavalry, and routed them. For ten minutes I was at close quarters with the enemy's infantry. Lieutenant Bickel fell upon his left flank, and some *yägers*, who had turned it, fell upon him in the rear; in short, the enemy was driven back, and we escaped a snare, in which we might have lost our lives or liberty. We took five officer's prisoners, (two of whom were Frenchmen who had served as volunteers), and about 60 men. The enemy lost many men; and we had three officers and about 50 killed and wounded. The enemy's detachment, which belonged to the Marquis de la Fayette's army, who was present himself, amounted to 1200 of his best men.

This example shews that courage and fortune alone saved us; for we had in every respect neglected the necessary precaution, by too much dependence upon the vicinity of our army. At any rate, during our rest, we ought to have sent small parties to *patrole* around, by which means timely intelligence of the enemy's approach would have been received: this was more especially necessary in a country like Virginia, which is so covered with forests, and where all the inhabitants were disaffected. If Major Macpherson had not committed the unpardonable fault of attacking too soon, the enemy would have had time to have inclined more to the left, by which we should have been cut off from the road to the army, and have been attacked on all sides.

If the enemy be defeated, you may indeed pursue, but this must be done very cautiously, and the country and particular circumstances well considered. If you have driven back a very superior force, and you suspect any stratagem, it is well to rest satisfied with the first advantage. Should you have this advantage over the enemy in hilly or woody countries, you must pursue him very cautiously, and not too far, for you run a risk of being cut off. But if the country be open that you can see around you, and you find that the enemy cannot be supported, you may in such a case pursue him until he is completely routed. For instance: in the affair at Spencer's Plantation, it would have been blameable had Colonel Simcoe followed the enemy; for our commission was fulfilled, and it was our duty to join the army again as soon as possible? Besides this, he would have run the risk of their being the advance guard of the enemy's army, which was following, (as was really the case) and would soon have supported them.

In order to find out and drive back the enemy's detachments, which may have rendered the country unsafe by their inroads, divide your corps into two or three parts, each of which ought to take a different route, that should one of them be attacked, the remainder may be ready for a support. By this disposition, you gain the advantage, that if the middle corps be fallen upon, the two others may attack the enemy's flank and rear. For instance: in the winter of 1778, when the

English army lay in Philadelphia, Colonel Wurmb frequently went out towards the enemy, who wintered at Valee's Forge, in order to cover the market people and tradesmen who furnished the army in Philadelphia with provisions. He generally divided his corps into three parts, one of which took the main road towards Lancaster, the second marched along Marschal's road, and the third took the great road down the Delaware, leading to Derby.

As these roads ran parallel, and only one or one and a half league from each other, the thickets and other covered places; which were between the three roads, could be so well searched by the lateral *patroles*, that no party of the enemy could be concealed here; each division had his appointed post, to halt, to lay in ambuscade for a certain time, with orders to support that party, which might happen to be attacked. General Morgan, who commanded a corps of riflemen and Indians, had frequently received orders from General Washington, to lay himself in ambuscade, in order to cut off one of our parties, or employ every means to attack and defeat it; but by reason of the very skilful marching order of Colonel Wurmb, this bold man never hazarded more than to shew himself at a distance.

In the seven years war, as the Prussian general. Von Driesen, returned from the Bamberg expedition to Hof, and encamped there, he received intelligence that a party of the enemy were approaching. Major Von Röhl, of Seculy's Hussars, received orders immediately to go against him with 300 hussars in the night. The Prussian major divided his detachment into three divisions, two of which turned sidewards, and the other he kept with him. At daybreak he met with one of the enemy's outposts, defeated it, together with the detachment who came to its assistance; on the pursuit, he met with a battalion of volunteers, who had posted themselves in bushes upon the height of Rehan. The Prussian major, perceiving this, halted, in order to wait for one of his detachments, one of which, commanded by Captain Ruhlman, he perceived advancing; he resolved the moment he saw that this battalion retreated in a square to attack them sword in hand, and he also completely routed it: as he was pursuing them he fell in with an Austrian regiment of hussars, whereupon he retreated in such good order, that the enemy did not even attempt to annoy him.

It sometimes happens, that you receive upon a march intelligence of a detachment that knows nothing of you, and has occupied a post close to yours; this is generally a good opportunity to surprise him, for very often, if they receive no intelligence of the enemy, they are too apt, during daytime, to forget the necessary precaution. I have seen, more than once, the men undress themselves, or stroll about immediately after a long march, in order to search for provisions, and the piquets, which were posted, not in much better preparation.—It is day! Nothing from the enemy! That was enough. The 19th English regiment once repented such a fault in Carolina. It was ordered to march to Charlestown; the commander thought himself sufficiently safe, as he was between the army and the before-mentioned fortress.

Upon the march he occupied a post, not far from Monckcornes, behind a small river, over which there was a bridge, placed a piquet on this side of the bridge, and had his two field pieces drawn in front of it. Major Armstrong, who was a good partisan, and who was skirmishing between the army and Charlestown, received information by his spies the moment that the English colonel had occupied this post. Though he had already made a long march, he took a handful of men, whose horses still appeared to be fresh; stole along through the woods as near the bridge as possible; galloped to it in the middle of the day, hewed down the piquet and many English soldiers in camp, the remainder were forced to take shelter in the neighbouring wood, and he returned without losing a man.

If sent out to destroy the magazines of the enemy, to take hostages or levy contributions, it must be done with the cavalry, for such duties must be performed expeditiously. In this case, it would be well to have mounted infantry, as I have before mentioned; for as you may be very distant from the army, the cavalry, covered always by infantry, can go double the distance, and be doubly secure. I advise you on such expeditions not to remain too long in one place, to halt always in the most covered countries when you wish to rest, and on your return to take a round-about way. For instance; as Prince Henry in 1758 invaded Franconia with the army from Vogtland, and the Prussian corps under General Driesen advanced to Bamberg, upon which the army of the empire had marched as far as Saaz in Bohemia in order to cover it: General Belling, then Lieutenant-Colonel, went with his hussars to Sarden and Konigwarth in the rear of the army of the empire, took hostages with him, and returned over Asch.

Immediately after he went again with his hussars in the country of Bamberg, as far as Kupferberg, from thence to Kemnat and Auterbach in the Upper Pfalz, and returned over Erbach, Forckheim and Bamberg, after taking a great number of hostages, and having spread terror and raised contribution through almost the whole of Franconia and Upper Pfalz.

This second example shews, that when such expeditions are undertaken with promptitude and precaution, they are generally successful. On 17th July, as the army under Lord Cornwallis during the Virginian campaigns stood at Suffolk, Colonel Dundas passed the Nansemond River with the 80th Scotch regiment of Foot, which had been mounted by permission of the commander in chief, turned the enemy's corps under General Barker, which stood behind Blackwater's River; destroyed an enemy's magazine in the neighbourhood of Edenton on the frontiers of North Carolina, and returned by Sommerton to the army on the 19th evening, having gone more than 100 miles.

If you find by good and trusty spies that a detachment of the enemy be on their march to attack you, and he has a *defilé* to pass, you must hasten to occupy it, and to conceal yourself in such a manner, that when he has pasted the *defilé* with a part of his men, (should he have forgotten the necessary precaution), you can fall upon him; but this must be done in the most sudden and resolute manner, for you will have it in your power to suffer as many of the enemy to come out of the *defilé* as you think proper to attack; whilst those in the rear cannot give the least assistance, but on the contrary will be thrown into confusion themselves, and be obliged to fly with the others. In this manner a few hundred cavalry will be a match for thousands, and even rout them.

But in this case the enemy should not be pursued farther than the *defilé*; for as his remaining men on the other side of the *defilé* will certainly form up, you would be falling into the same snare yourself, and lose all your former advantage.

For instance, had Colonel Dundas followed this rule, and gone to meet the Duke de Lauzun as far as the *defilé* near Porwell's Mill, instead of waiting for him at Saul's Plantation, near Gloucester, he would certainly have overcome the French hussars; and supposing the duke to have used the greatest precaution in passing the *defilé*, our retreat would have always been safe, having light infantry with us, and the greatest part of the road to Gloucester being woody.

There are circumstances in war, which must be performed in such haste, that cavalry alone can be employed: but as you may be forced to return the same way, and have to risk yourself in the same *defilés* through which you went, such *defilés* ought to be occupied with light infantry, in order to secure your rear, and prevent being cut off by the enemy. For instance, as Lord Cornwallis in the Virginian campaign marched on the 20th June from New Kent Court-house towards Williamsburg, and wished to conceal his march from the Marquis de la Fayette who stood near Richmond, he ordered Colonel Simcoe to manoeuvre towards Newcastle, which lay behind Richmond, in order to attract the enemy's attention to that quarter; the colonel had with him his own regiment, the *yäger's* detachment, and the mounted riflemen; but on his route to the Black and Matadequin Rivers, (upon the left bank of the latter of which there is an extensive *defilé*, which he was forced to leave in his rear, having no other way to choose for his return, and especially as the *defilé* of Matadequin lay in a direct line with Richmond, where the enemy was) the colonel sent me with a grenadier and a light infantry company together with the *yägers* behind the first, and Major Armstrong, with the Ranger's battalion, to stand behind the latter, in order to cover both passes.

As the road from Richmond to Newcastle entered the road from Williamsburg, at the pass of Matadequin River, I posted for security Captain Stauvensand upon this road some miles on my left towards Richmond; I had also posted an officer with 30 *yägers* in a thicket upon the great road, some miles off between the pass where Major Armstrong stood and myself. The enemy's party fell upon both my advance posts, but being repulsed with loss, they gave up the attempt: towards evening Colonel Simcoe, who had taken an American colonel prisoner in a skirmish, returned, and we joined the army about midnight at Baun's Plantation.

If you have the advance guard of an army, or of a corps that is appointed to invest a fortress, you must as soon as you are a few leagues from it hasten your march as much as possible, in order to arrive before the place unexpectedly, and rush into the suburbs, where you will probably surprise many officers and men. The commander of the fortress may perhaps have committed a fault, and suffered the cattle to graze near town until the last moment, which will thus fall into your hands, and occasion a scarcity in the town a few days sooner, only you must not pay any attention to the firing from the ramparts, which will certainly take place; for as your army is following, and certainly seen by the enemy from the steeples, you may be assured that he will not send out any troops against you, left such troops should be driven back, and you press with them at the same time into the town.

If the enemy be routed, or he retreats so fast that you cannot come up with him, be doubly on your guard, and not half intoxicated with your good fortune, for you cannot tell what kind of an opponent you have to deal with. The following example will support this rule. It was during the war which Charles the Twelfth, king of Sweden, carried on with the Russians and Augustus, king of Poland; this hero in the campaign of 1701 had already made himself master of Courland, and sent his detachment as far as the Polish territory, in order to protect; Prince Sapicha against Oginsky, who had openly declared against the king of Sweden, and attacked and routed several detachments of the Swedish army. The king resolved to find out, attack, and destroy this enemy.

For this purpose he ordered on the 1st of December, in the night, a detachment of 400 men of the foot guards to be conveyed in sledges, entered Courland, and joined Colonel Humerhielm, who was posted with a detachment of cavalry at Schandau. The march was continued from Schandau to Calivaria, to which place ——— Meyerfeld, then stationed at Polangen, was ordered. The king, who here received intelligence that the enemy was at Skudi hastened to it with the cavalry; but the enemy had left Skudi in great haste, and retired farther off. The king resolved to wait for the infantry at Skudi, and leaving it behind him in this town, hastened on the following day towards Tirksel, which place Oginsky had only left a few minutes when the king arrived, and had taken his route to Tirsky. The king pursued him thither, but still not finding him as expected, he gave up all hopes of meeting with him.

As the troops were now weary, and wanted rest, the king ordered them to be quartered in the town, and he himself occupied the castle, where for safety a guard of only 30 cavalry was posted. Oginsky, who was instantly informed by the priest of the town of the security of the Swedes, took 6000 men in the night, and hastened to Tirsky, in order to surprise them. He found it open, galloped into it with a loud shout as far as the market place, where he set fire to some houses, in order to increase the confusion of the Swedes. The Swedes, who had not in the least expected such a visit, and had gone to bed, awoke, and took up arms with such precipitation, that many of them appeared on horseback in their very shirts. Captain Sack, and Count Flemming of the horse guards were the first who came on horseback; they collected a handful of men, and attacked the Poles with the greatest courage, which resolution gave the remainder of the Swedes time to collect themselves, and support the attack. The Poles were attacked on all sides and driven back. The Swedes fell so furiously upon them, that great numbers of Poles were cut to pieces or taken; Oginsky's own horse and a pair of kettle-drums fell into the hands of the brave Swedes.

In this instance, the manner in which Oginsky executed his excellent plan, is as much to blame as the security of Charles the 12th; had the former silently occupied the avenues and streets around the quarters of the Swedes, and sent a strong detachment to the castle, where the first attack ought to have been made, his success must have been certain; especially being so far superior in number. The Swedes would have been cut to pieces one by one as they came out of the houses, the king taken prisoner, and the Polish general would have had the honour of having put an end to the war.

SECTION 2
OF THE CHOICE OF A POST IN THE FIELD.

Whatever may be the object of an outpost, all the rules laid down for this branch of service have the same tendency: *viz.* to beware against insult, and adopt such measures as will render even the best plan of the enemy abortive.

Outposts, where light troops are generally employed, are intended for covering an army or corps and to secure it from surprise. They are calculated to observe an enemy laying opposite, or at a short distance, attend to his motions, and send to headquarters a satisfactory report of every circumstance which may be discovered; and in the mean time, should the enemy commit himself in any respect, the outposts will endeavour to seize the opportunity and execute a *coup de main*.

This will prove, how vigilant and cautious outposts should be, as the safety of the whole army, and the lives and liberty of thousands rest upon them.

The first rule for the commander of a light corps who arrives at a post which he knows only by the map, will be to march to some commanding ground, and there leave the men under arms until he receive intelligence of the enemy; for which purpose he should send small parties of cavalry to all the avenues leading to the enemy; these will collect information in the neighbouring villages, and bring back with them some of the principal inhabitants.

The commanding officer should endeavour to get from these people the intelligence he wants; he should enquire about all the issues which may lead towards the enemy, at what distance he is, how strong, and how far he sends his *patroles*, in order not to forget this last point, he ought to mark the names of such places upon his map. He should ask those inhabitants who appear friendly inclined to recommend some trusty man to serve as a spy, upon being well paid. He should besides, procure the best guides, ride with them about the country, place his posts, and let the men off duty rest themselves, and cook their victuals. Infantry may be suffered to take off their accoutrements, and the cavalry to unbridle and feed their horses; but no man is to be permitted to pull off his clothes, or go out of camp.

Guards of cavalry must be placed in the open country, where *vedettes* can command an extensive prospect; and centinels be planted in the thickest cover, though in such a manner as to be able to discover their front and flanks at some distance. If the ground permit, *vedettes* and sentries ought to be advanced as far as eight hundred or a thousand paces. During the night the guards of cavalry must retire and take post behind those of infantry. Riflemen should perform the day, and light infantry the night duty, or act together mixed. If it can be done and the ground allow it, *vedettes* and sentries should be posted during the night so as to have high ground before them, as an object is far more easily discerned at night from below, than in looking down from an hill. If there be in the neighbourhood a wood crossed by any roads leading to the enemy, or any *defilé* near the posts through which the enemy can approach undiscovered; in either case the piquets must be advanced to these places; but should the post you are ordered to take be ill chosen, and should you find a much better within about a thousand paces, occupy the latter by all means, taking care to acquaint the general with it.

For instance, in Lord Cornwallis's retreat from Suffolk to Portsmouth, an officer of the staff planted me with a detachment of cavalry and infantry, between a thick wood and a river, the banks of which were swampy on both sides, with a dyke and bridge across. As I had been wounded in that very place, five months before in a skirmish, and fortunately for me knew the country better than he; I retreated over the dyke, reported the circumstance to headquarters, and my conduct was approved.

In another instance; when General Sir H. Clinton made his retreat from Philadelphia, through the Jerseys in the year 1778, and wished to pass the Ankocus by Fostertown, along which river the enemy had ruined all the bridges; I was sent over with 150 *yägers*, to take post and cover the working parties which were to repair the bridge. The place where I had been sent was a plain, surrounded at the distance of a league with woods and heights, under the cover of which, the enemy could have approached unperceived and attacked me unawares. I placed my posts as I had been ordered, but taking with me an officer and 30 men proceeded to the summit of the highest hill, in order to reconnoitre the country around; from thence I perceived at the distance of half a league, a few houses and a mill, and by examining my map I concluded that it was a place called Carstown, situated upon an arm of the Ankocus.

I sent for 30 *yägers* more, and having approached the place I saw that the bridge upon that arm had also been ruined. The mill was occupied by a small party of riflemen, who gave way after a few shots, when they saw that I was determined to carry the post. I contrived to cross the river upon the ruins of the bridge, occupied the mill and reported my conduct; upon which I received orders to continue where I was; I was reinforced with 30 *yägers* more, the bridge repaired during the night, and the general did me the honour to acknowledge that I had gained for him a day's march.

If the enemy be near, the best way (supposing the rear to be well covered,) will be to draw the outposts as near as possible to those of the enemy; they will thereby cover more effectually the intended ground; the men will be more alert, having the enemy in sight, his motions will be more easily watched, and a better opportunity given to profit by any fault he may commit. General Luckner always acted in this manner during the seven years war; the Duke of Lauzun by Gloucester in Virginia, would by this means have been of great service to the corps under General Choisy, if Lord Cornwallis had attempted so fight his way out of York, on that side with the remnant of his army, as was in fact the original intention of this brave general.

Placing piquets and centinels is not to be considered as the only method for protecting an outpost; *patroles* must also be frequently sent towards the enemy in order to procure timely intelligence of his motions and approach; these must be, especially, during the night, incessantly backwards and forwards upon the roads which lead in that direction and cross each other before the line of *vedettes* and sentries. If the country be so intersected that the posts cannot see far before them, or a *defilé*, be so situated in front, that it cannot be conveniently occupied, and might offer an opportunity to the enemy to approach undiscovered, it would be proper to prepare in the night-time an ambuscade of a non-commissioned officer and a few *yägers*, with orders to give a volley as soon as they should hear a party of the enemy approaching.

Supposing that it should occasion the loss of a man or two; so inconsiderable a loss is not adequate to the immense advantage which would result from this measure; and if the *yägers* be properly trained, it will but seldom happen. I cannot recollect more than one instance during the seven campaigns of the American war, where an ambuscade of this kind was lost. It happened near Portsmouth on the 19th of March 1781, when General Arnold was informed that the Marquis de la Fayette was marching against him with a strong corps; in order to be acquainted in time with the approach of that corps, I placed a non-commissioned officer and 6 *yägers* in ambuscade at about half a league upon the road which the enemy was to take, two of whom fell into his hands, but the Hessian and Anspach *yägers* were so well trained to this kind of warfare, that they were equal to the artful Croats, and even these two would not have been taken prisoners, if, out of eagerness to shoot some of the enemy, they had not suffered his advance guard to approach them too near.

Such ambuscades are principally useful in an enemy's country where the inhabitants are unfriendly towards you; and it will prevent the enemy from shooting or carrying off sentries in which the American militia were as great adepts as the Croats; it secures so effectually your posts against parties of the enemy, that they will not afterwards approach them without fear.

Strong *patroles* of infantry and cavalry ought also to be sent out daily towards the enemy, especially before daybreak, *but not at any fixed hour*, in order to disappoint or make him suffer, if he should attempt to surprise any of your small *patroles*.

Whole companies or troops may also, now and then, be posted in covered countries, between the outposts and the enemy, and fall unawares upon such parties as may approach.

If you be frequently alarmed by the enemy, do not suffer it quietly, but alarm him still more frequently, in order to keep him in awe, and tire him out.

During the daytime, the men are in general to be allowed as much rest as circumstances will admit, especially if the country be open around you; cavalry may then be permitted to unbridle and unsaddle for a moment to ease the horses, and infantry to take off their accoutrements, but not to straggle out of camp without leave. Before sunset cavalry must bridle and infantry put on their accoutrements; but should the enemy be near, cavalry must always remain bridled; and at the time of feeding, one half must be ready to mount on horseback, and so on by turns; during the night, half of the cavalry must mount alternately, and half of the infantry remain under arms in the same manner.

If you arrive in the night time at a post within a short distance from the enemy, and be unacquainted with the country, you should remain on the spot under arms, and detach small parties of a non-commissioned officer and 4 or 6 men towards the front and flanks to the distance of four or five hundred paces; a few of these men must be sent two or three times every hour, four or five hundred paces still farther, halt and listen attentively; they must be ordered to fire as soon as they perceive the enemy, and at the moment one of these small parties fires, the whole chain must do the same; this cannot fail to embarrass even a strong enemy should he be approaching.

This once liberated the two first *yäger* companies from a night attack of the enemy, at Rariton-landing, in New-Jersey. In the winter of the beginning of 1777, the American Colonel Butler and Major Otterndorf, who were posted with a strong corps, about a league from Rariton-landing, formed the plan of carrying the two companies at once from three different sides, in the night time, as the frequent attempts they had made upon my post, which formed a projecting angle out of the chain, had always miscarried; the division which arrived on the right of Quietel-town, and which intended to have penetrated between Captain Wreden's post and mine, was discovered first; the sentries fired, and as I had a few weeks before, given orders that when a sentry fired, the whole chain should; fortunately for us they all fired; the two other American divisions thought that they had also been discovered, gave up the attempt and retired quietly.

The officers and non-commissioned officers of Grand Guards and piquets, must be pointedly informed of what they have to do; they must especially be strictly ordered to report without delay to the commander of the corps whatever they may have observed.

Such intelligence as may be received from deserters or spies is not to be despised and neglected, though apparently improbable; an officer will do well to prepare in consequence, especially if he have to deal with a cunning and enterprising enemy, for one of this description will never follow the beaten tract of stratagems, but act in a manner wholly new and unexpected. The loss of the important post at Stony-point, was entirely owing to the obstinacy of the commanding officer, who despised the information given him the day before by the inhabitants: in the same year and from the same cause the enemy would have succeeded in the attack upon Paul's-hook, if the American Colonel Lee had been as enterprising as General Vane; for the commander of Paul's-hook had treated the notice of the intended attack upon his post with the same contempt as the former.

A light corps is frequently posted in order to secure the communication between two armies, or between an army, a strong detachment, and a fortified town; or, to prevent that communication between two armies or fortified towns of the enemy and intercept his convoys.

For instance; in the first case, when Lord Cornwallis marched through both the Carolinas, finding himself too far from Charlestown to preserve a communication with that place, which was absolutely necessary for him, he left Colonel Cruger with a corps of light troops at Sixtynine.

In the second case, towards the end of the campaign of 1757, when Prince Charles of Lorraine followed the Duke of Bevern into Silesia, whilst the King of Prussia was in Saxony, General Haddick was sent with a body of Croats and hussars to observe the motions of the king, as it was probable that he would hasten to the relief of Silesia, General Haddick therefore took post at Grossenhayn behind the Röder whence he could at all times watch the motions of the king; Frederick advanced, and General Haddick having acquainted the imperial army in Silesia with the approach of the king, retired before him to Bohemia, through Konigsbruck, Bautzen, and Luben.

2ndly. During the siege of Olmutz, Colonel Lanius had taken post with 150 Croats and hussars near Friedland and Lobnik, upon the road from Neis to Olmutz, and having received information that General Fouquet was on his march from Neis to Olmutz with a strong convoy, he attacked, during the night, the division commanded by General Puttkammer; but the vigilance of the Prussian infantry was such that he was obliged to retire after an unsuccessful attempt. A short time afterwards he was more fortunate upon the same ground, having gained the woods and heights near Teutchlodniss, he fell upon two free corps (Lenoble and Salenmon) in the *defilé* of Lebenhusen, upon the Prussian line of communication, and took a few pieces of artillery and about 300 prisoners.

The enemy will certainly employ every means in his power to overtake and destroy such detachments; they must therefore be the more vigilant; as long as the season of the year permit, they ought never to return to the same place at night, but move as often as possible, and procure good spies who will give timely information; they must not, however, lose sight of the object in view, and above all secure their retreat, for fear of being cut off.

For instance, suppose that our army occupy Fulda, and this place be blockaded or besieged by an enemy who receives his convoys from Hanau or Aschaffenburg, as he could not occupy Gelnhausen on account of its natural position, half surrounded with high mountains, I am detached there, in order to annoy him upon the road, from Hanau to Aschaffenburg; admitting that the Wetterau be in our possession and the country of Mayntz in our favour: being so situated, I would procure spies in Gelnhausen, Salmunster, Hanau, and about Aschaffenburg and Dettingen, to be informed when the enemy should send convoys by water from Aschaffenburg to Hanau, and when these should be transported from Hanau to Fulda: I would change my position every night and let no one be informed of it but my principal spy, who should live in Gelnhausen and transmit to me the intelligence which he may receive from the other spies: I would successively occupy the following positions:

Firstly, Durich near Gelnhausen;

Secondly, The wood between Wachtersbach and the great farm;

Thirdly, In the rear of Breitenborn;

Fourthly, In the wood of Budingen near Hunerhof; and;

Fifthly, By the Abt's Ecke.

From this last, (which I should not occupy often) I would make inroads with small parties to the very gates of Hanau, and carry off officers from the *promenades*; but as soon as my *coup de main* should have been performed, I would withdraw to Nidda, Hungen, or even farther; approach the road of Fulda by Gedern once more, remain for a few nights between Salmunster and Steinau, and watch another opportunity: this country being much covered with woods and hills, it is impossible that the enemy could ever completely surround me; whatever appears impossible to the generality of men, is always the easier in the execution. If one of my spies inform me that a large convoy of the enemy be going from Aschaffenburg to Hanau, I would go towards the mountains, cross them between Haitz and the Kaltenborn, pass the River Kintzig at Höchst, approach the right bank of the Mayn through the Spessart, and endeavour to burn the convoy; if I should fail in my enterprise, I would destroy all the boats I could on the banks of the Mayn; this alone would be sufficient, as it would greatly augment the enemy's difficulty, in transporting forage or provisions, and of course harass his troops by forcing him to protect all his convoys with strong detachments.

There is in fact, very little danger attending expeditions of this kind; for, you arrive at a place of safety before the enemy's troops in the country are informed of it, and can march in consequence. In this instance, in order the better to conceal my retreat from the enemy, who would probably send strong detachments from Hanau on both sides of the Kintzig as far as Gelnhausen and Salmunster to intercept my party, I would direct my retreat, through the Spessart, inclining to the right towards Bieber and Orberreissig, cross the Kintzig near Schluchtern and endeavour to regain the Wetterau. Should I be informed that the enemy be preparing to send a convoy from Hanau, I would remain as privately as possible in the country where I was, that the enemy might not be informed of my position. I would march off during the night, cross the Kintzig near Offenau, Wertheim or Höchst, and remain in the woody mountains behind Orb, from thence, send my spies out to ascertain when the convoy would arrive in the vicinity of Altenhaslau (I must suppose that the convoy will march upon Meerholtz in order to avoid the *defilé* of Gelnhausen) as soon as I received certain intelligence, I would approach Salmunster, with two thirds of my corps and make a resolute attack upon the head of the escort at the moment of their entering this district, whilst they were separated from the others by the *defilés* of Auffenau and Höchst.

With the remaining third of my corps I would send small detachments to annoy the escort between Auffenau and Höchst, and to kill a few waggoners and horses in order to encrease confusion. If I should have the good fortune to rout the escort, I would endeavour to destroy horses and waggons as much as possible, and again retire to the Wetterau, through Salmunster, Birstein, Wenings, and Gedern; should I be unsuccessful and even completely routed, I should be always sure of escaping, as the enemy would not pursue being wholly occupied for the safety of his convoy. At all events, that woody and mountainous country would favour my retreat.

Should I, on the contrary, have to defend a country from such inroads of an enemy, I would exert my utmost to defeat his purposes, and act upon the defensive according to the same rules I mentioned for the offensive. For instance, when General Washington was with his army in the year 1779 near Chatham, to cover the province of New Jersey, he detached Colonel White with a light corps in order to check the incursions of General Sir H. Clinton into the province of New York and observe his motions; he seldom remained more than twenty-four hours in one place; he was sometimes at Bedford, at Newcastle, Cinq Cinq, and frequently fell, unawares, upon the outposts of the English. He preserved such a secrecy, that even the people of the country, who were all in his favour, never knew where he was.

For instance; we had not heard of him for some time, and I was sent to him under a pretence with a flag of truce; I rode the whole day, in quest of him without being able to hear anything of him from the inhabitants of the country, when I fell at once into one of his parties, delivered my message, received the answer and returned as much in the dark as before respecting the place of his abode. The same artifice was once more used for the same purpose, and the officer who had been sent, after as fruitless a research as mine, met him on his return, near our outposts which he had alarmed early in the morning.

An officer when he occupies a post, must be particularly attentive to secure his rear. If circumstances should force him to leave a bridge or *defilé* of any kind behind him, he must not fail to occupy it with a detachment of infantry and send frequent *patroles* on that side.

If the post be on the bank of a river for the defence of a bridge, it will be necessary to place some outposts as far as possible on the other side of the river, that the enemy cannot come unawares; if the post be occupied during a few days, it would be proper to raise a *flêche* for the defence of the bridge; if time do not allow it, a few large trees may be placed *en abatis* across the bridge, or some waggons, observing to take off their wheels on one side: the number and situation of the fords in the neighbourhood must be ascertained, and harrows thrown into them to impede the enemy's passage. Small posts must be placed along the river, and *patroles* cross each other constantly on this side of the river.

If the season of the year do not permit you to keep the field any longer, and the troops must be cantoned, or occupy winter quarters, self-convenience is the last thing to be attended to; the largest barns must be filled with as many horses as they can contain, observing the usual precautions, that the horses can be taken out in a moment The light infantry must be lodged as crowded as possible in the houses nearest to the issues, and these be stopped with waggons. Two alarm posts must be appointed, one for the day and the other for the night. The first may be in the front or on the sides of the village, observing that the light infantry occupy the gardens and hedges; but the second must be in the rear of the village in order to avoid being circumscribed in your movements, as you cannot see from what quarter the enemy advance.

As light troops are, in general, calculated for procuring information, in case of retreat you aft according to the intelligence you receive from them; but without precipitation, for it maybe a false alarm and hurt your character.

Is the post to be maintained in case of attack and the troops quartered in the neighbourhood have orders to support it? In this case, the issues ought to be stopped as completely as possible with trees and casks filled with dung; the *yägers* take post behind this kind of intrenchment and hedges, and in such cases the cavalry ought to be made to fight on foot, or placed where it be less exposed to the enemy's fire, in order to repulse such as would attempt to penetrate, or to be in readiness to make a sally on the arrival of succours and fall upon the enemy in his retreat. Between the issues that have been stopped, openings ought to be made in the hedges and masked with bushes, through these sally out by whole platoons of infantry and cavalry upon the enemy at his onset: whatever is unexpected strikes the mind with fear, and where you hazard most, most is to be gained.

The brave Lieutenant Colonel Maitland, by birth a Scotchman, who had already lost his right hand in an action at sea against the French, and nevertheless went, through the hardships of the duties of the English light infantry, preserved in this manner Stony-ferry in South Carolina; with only 500 British and Hessians, he repulsed the attack of General Lincoln with 3000 Americans; Lieutenant Kuhne of the Hessian grenadiers signalized himself there in one of the sallies.

Should you receive from your spies, a certain information, that the enemy intend a *coup de main* upon your post during the night, you must endeavour to lay a snare for him. For instance, let him approach as near as possible, and then falling furiously upon him from every quarter, cut down as many as you can, and retire to your post.

Half of the corps may also be placed in ambuscade, at half a league, on the right or left of the road upon which the enemy are to come; and whilst he attacks the post, these will fall upon his flank or rear. For example:—In the winter of 1762, the Austrian Colonel D'Alton, who was posted at Reichenbach in Silesia, had laid a plan to surprise the Prussian detachment, commanded by Pritwitz, which occupied Rothensieben; but the latter had information of it, and placing himself in ambuscade with his detachment, upon the road, fell unawares upon Colonel D'Alton on his march, routed him, and took above a hundred prisoners,

Should you receive certain intelligence that the enemy intend a surprise upon your post, and be also assured of the road he will take; march at the same time by another road upon his own post, carry off all he may have left in it, observing to follow, on your return, the road by which the enemy went, and which, according to the principles of the art of war, he will not certainly take on his return: General Luckner once made use of this stratagem against Colonel Fisher's corps during the seven year's war.

Light troops are also employed in sieges, to blockade those sides of the besieged town upon which the real attack is not intended; on this duty, the commander of a light corps, must be particularly vigilant to guard against any sally the garrison may attempt for the purpose of procuring provisions from the neighbouring villages; under these circumstances the night posts of the light corps ought to be placed as near as possible to the town, the corps itself be under arms during each night, and at least one half remain accoutred and the horses bridled in the day time, in order to be always ready to fall upon the sally and repulse it; this must be done in the most resolute and furious manner, and sacrifice everything rather than suffer the enemy to succeed in his intentions; for the few heads of horned cattle he might thus procure, would probably retard the fall of the place two or three days longer, if the garrison be small and the commandant resolute.

In the second siege of Cassel, the Brunswick, Turkish corps, occupied the Waldau and Bettenhausen; in the middle of the day the French made a sally upon these villages whilst the herds were grazing in the meadows, and succeeded in driving them into the town, because the Turkish corps was not ready to check the sally as it ought to have been. When you occupy such a post before the garrison is completely blockaded and prevented from going out of its gates, the best plan will be to order the peasants to drive their cattle to some villages in the rear, or forbid fending them to graze at all; for, if you be in an enemy's country the inhabitants may easily have previously agreed with the commandant to graze their cattle as near as possible to the town; and as, in such circumstances, they look upon them as lost, it is not improbable that they should prefer their falling into the hands of friends.

Before I conclude this section, I will offer for instruction one more example respecting the country about Gelnhausen: It is the winter expedition of 1761, under Prince Ferdinand, when, in the beginning of February, the Allies fell unawares out of Westphalia upon the French, and advanced upon Cassel, Ziegenhayn, and Marburg, whilst a flying corps under the Hereditary Prince of Brunswick entered the Wetterau, and the parties of his light troops spread themselves over the country, as far as the gates of Hanau, into the cantonments of that part of the French army which had collected near Bergen. General Luckner, who covered the left wing of the corps commanded by the Hereditary Prince, advanced as far as Gelnhausen, which was occupied by Count Chabot, who retreated upon the Spessart at the approach of the Allies. Before he advanced further through Budingen, the Hereditary Prince had left a corps at Bierstein, in order to favour his or General Luckner's retreat should it become necessary.

When the latter had found Gelnhausen abandoned by the enemy, he took his quarters in it, and remained perfectly quiet, day and night, in this town, whose inhabitants were far from being well affected to the Allies: this conduct appears the more surprising from so celebrated a *partisan*, especially as he knew Count Chabot to be a man of great military talents; he had, however, covered his front and right flank; but according to what information I have obtained in the country, he had entirely neglected the bridges of Hoechst, Wertheim and Auffenau: had Count Chabot been more enterprising, and had he passed the Kintzig by Höchst or Auffenau, with the greater part of his corps, and placed himself in ambuscade between the Glasshütte and Gelnhausen, whilst one of his parties might have made a false attack upon Luckner's outposts about Altenhaslau, the latter must have been undone, having no retreat left but upon Birstein, and a long chain of *defilés* in his rear: Count Chabot would, in fact, have risked nothing in this enterprise, as no one could have cut off his retreat upon the Spessart.

I was also informed that a gentleman in Gelnhausen had acquainted Count Chabot with the imprudent security of General Luckner, and that he had, in consequence of this information, advanced to Grossenhausen to attack Luckner, but, fortunately for the latter, an officer of Count Chabot's corps who attempted to seize upon an inhabitant of Eichhof, probably for a guide, had been so careless as to suffer the farmer to escape; General Luckner being acquainted by him with the danger he was in, quitted Gelnhausen instantly, and retreated expeditiously upon Birstein.

This example will prove, how dangerous it is to shut oneself up in a place, especially one like Gelnhausen, which forms a true *cul de sac.* Supposing even that, on account of the rigour of the season, the Hanoverian General was obliged to put his men under cover, could not he have done it during the day only? But it being in the month of March, his men living in plenty, and especially as the place was not capable of defence, and he was not to remain long in it, he could very well have left it every night, and have occupied the wood of Breitenborn; in this case he wanted only an outpost at the Glasshütte, and another about Kaltenborn;. the first, for fending *patroles* on this side of the Kintzig from Höchst till above Auffenau, and the second would have performed the same duty over the Gettenbach towards Hanau; he could, moreover, have placed a day post of *avertissement,* on the top of the tower in Gelnhausen, and another in the vineyards out of the Haitzer gate; besides, I should always prefer the post of Breitenbach to that of Gelnhausen, because from the latter place I could have an equal command over the whole country, by sending out detachments, and be safe on my rear.

If a partisan have reason to suppose that a general engagement will soon occur between both armies, he must endeavour to post himself in such a manner, that he may, during the action, turn the rear of the enemy and fall upon their baggage or stores. Whatever be the fate of the battle, if he be enterprising, he can greatly hurt the enemy; at such a time, he has nothing to fear from the enemy's partisans, for, during a battle, they are on the flanks, or at a very little distance from their army, ready to cover the retreat in case of bad success, or to improve victory and annoy the retreat of the vanquished enemy. For instance:—Could not a Luckner or a Scheider have attempted, during the night before the Battle of Bergen, to penetrate as far as the heights between Homburg and Frankfurth, which is a very woody and covered country, and while the armies were engaged, could not he have rapidly advanced close upon Frankfurth, and carried off or destroyed the field equipage of the French, or whatever he might have met with?

Who knows what might have happened if the French had heard, during the battle, the news of such an event in their rear? At least it could have been attempted without danger; for the whole of the French army was at Bergen, the garrison of Frankfurth would certainly not have risked itself out of the gates, and whatever might have been the result, a partisan was sure to make his retreat good by inclining towards the right. For instance: during the Battle of Soor, gained by the King of Prussia over the Austrians, the Croats fell upon the rear of the Prussian army, and carried off the king's chancery, and part of the baggage of that army. Another instance of this kind occurred during the Battle of Prague; the Austrian General Beck, with a corps of Croats, turned also the Prussian army, carried sword in hand the town of Prandeis, which was garrisoned by a Prussian battalion for the protection of the camp equipage, killed a great number, took upwards of 600 prisoners, besides several pairs of colours, and, loaded with booty, happily made his retreat upon General Daun's army, after having destroyed the bridge upon the Elbe.

Did not the Croats use the same manoeuvre against Gustavus Adolphus, during the Battle of Lutzen? and it must be observed, that the greatest partisans that ever existed belonged to that nation. I will here give a fourth example:—Whilst the French army and the Allies were in presence of each other by Minden, General Freitag was near Hameln with the Hanoverian *yägers*; he foresaw the battle, marched privately towards Detmold, and carried off a whole column of French camp equipage, which they were sending back immediately after the battle.—These examples will prove that success will always favour the bold, and indeed there is hardly anything impossible to the commander of a well-disciplined light corps, if he have but courage and judgment; only he must not follow the beaten track if he wishes to obtain uncommon success.

SECTION 3
OF INCLOSED POSTS

These posts being in general calculated for resisting a *coup de main*, an officer entrusted with such a command, must take every precaution to secure it from surprise; for, if the post be part of the chain of winter cantonments, or intended for covering a communication, it renders it of such importance, that the last man must be sacrificed for its defence. On arriving at a post of this kind, the first thing will be to assemble the principal inhabitants, or the municipality, and procure every information respecting the place, and whether there be any concealed issues, particularly if a river pass through or near the place: for example—the Kintzig runs between the suburb and the town of Gelnhausen, and forms an island at the upper part of the town near the castle; if the garrison, in time of war, were to think themselves perfectly secure on that side, being covered by the river, an artful enemy could easily make them suffer for it; for the river is fordable for men and horses at the place where it divides into two arms and forms an island, and the town may be entered through the mills.

The commanding officer must, immediately after his arrival, take a ride round the place, within as well as without, and observe whether the enemy can approach undiscovered from any quarter, and what side of the wall be less capable of defence. If you suspect the inhabitants, you will do well to secure some of the principal, more especially those who have the most influence in the place; they must; be guarded in their own houses, and the inhabitants informed that, in case of treachery, these hostages will be put to death; they may also be forced, in case of necessity, to recommend certain people to serve as spies, and be made answerable for them.

But after having shewn this severity for your own safety; you must also assure the inhabitants that you will maintain discipline among your soldiers; and that every indulgence will be granted, which their behaviour may deserve.

The municipality must be ordered to require from the inhabitants an immediate delivery of their arms and ammunition; the bells must never be suffered to be rung, and no person to leave the town without permission from the commandant; every housekeeper must be informed that he is personally answerable, with his life, for every person of his family, and even for his lodgers: as soon as it begins to be dark, no person is to go in the streets without light, and except in case of absolute necessity, no one, whoever he may be, shall be in the streets after nine o'clock; no public solemnities or diversions must be allowed; and in case of an alarm, lights must be placed in the windows of the first and second floor, but nobody attempt to go out of doors; innkeepers must be ordered to send to the main-guard every day the names and the business of every person they lodge, from whence they come, and where they go. All these orders must be given in writing to the municipality, that ignorance may be no excuse for disobedience.

A main-guard must be fixed upon, about the centre of the town, guards placed at every gate, and a small post on the highest steeple (I would recommend trusty non-commissioned officers to be employed for this last duty); the men must be quartered as comfortably as possible, night alarm posts appointed for each half company or company, towards the issues of the place; cavalry must be ordered, in this case, to fall in near the main-guard; every officer in the garrison must know perfectly where his company or platoon is to fall in. If some parts of the walls of the place Should not permit the men to stand upon them and fire, a rampart walk must be made up with thick planks laid upon trestles, waggons, or upon casks, observing, that where sentries are to be planted, the place must be raised a little higher in order to command a more extensive view.

In the daytime, sentries may be planted singly, but during the night doubled, and so situated, that nothing can steal unperceived between them: should these walls be so high, that the temporary walks cannot be made without much labour and time, the upper part of the wall must be pulled down towards the inside, and the rampart walk built with the stones. The parapet ought not to be raised higher than up to the mid-body of the soldier, for should it be higher, the men are liable to conceal themselves too much behind it, and fire in the air, in order to be less exposed; and you must endeavour to persuade them that parapets are not intended as a cover from the enemy's fire, but merely as an obstacle to the enemy.

All the gates but one, or at most two, must be stopped up; it is in general done with litter heaped up so high, that a man can hardly creep out above it. Gates may also be stopped with casks filled up with litter, which will be more convenient to remove, should it be necessary. These gates which are intended for the passage in and out, are to be blocked up at night, or when thought necessary, in such a manner as to be easily opened again: the best way is to use an abatis, *viz.* whole trees with their branches, the ends of which must be cut sharp, and a little burned to make them harder; thus prepared, the trees are brought to the gateway, the branches outwards, and the trunks forming a cross one upon the other, and made fast by strong wooden hooks driven in the ground, in order to prevent the enemy from dragging them off; apple trees are preferable.

It is very proper to dig traverses behind such gates as may be used occasionally, for should the enemy succeed in forcing them, he may be stopped there.

If there be any towers over the gates, they must be sufficiently occupied in case of an attack, and their access well defended; a large quantity of stones and heavy blocks of wood must also be at hand to throw upon such as may attempt to make themselves masters of the gate, and other heaps placed at certain distances, in case the, enemy should offer to storm; where the wall be fallen, the breach must be filled up by an abatis, or with strong pieces of timber planted close to each other, and deeply sunk into the ground.

Should there be in the town, a castle or a large church, somewhat asunder from the houses, it may be used as a citadel for the last place of retreat; the streets at some distance around it must be stopped with traverses and *trous de loups*. and every possible obstacle thrown in the enemy's way, to embarrass his pursuit through the streets. Breastworks must be erected across the meeting of streets, in order to dispute every inch of ground in the town, even after the walls have been forced. If you be in an enemy's country where you suspect treason, you can fill up some houses, near the principal issues, with straw and other materials that will easily catch fire, and threaten the inhabitants that you are resolved to burn the town, should the enemy succeed in surprising you.

This preserved me once during the American war. Immediately after the taking of Trenton by the enemy, Colonel Donop, who bad occupied Montholy with the 42nd regiment, two Hessian grenadier battalions, and the *yäger* company under my command, was obliged to quit precipitately this post, in order to gain the passage of Croswick, which secured his communication with Prince Town, where General Grant was with his corps. In order to secure his march, at least on one side, the colonel, who had every reason to expect that the enemy would molest his retreat, ordered me to remain in Montholy with ninety men, Highlanders, Hessian grenadiers and riflemen, and to defend myself to the last man, or at least to hold out till midnight. I unroofed the two bridges upon the river which went through the town, but which was fordable a little higher up; for the last resource I assembled the inhabitants, ordered everyone to remain in his house, and swore that if I were attacked tacked by the enemy, or they should offer to rise against me, I would before leaving it set the town on fire; I knew that the greater part of the inhabitants were disaffected, and had concealed arms and ammunition: my threats succeeded, the Americans, who were afraid to see this commercial town reduced to ashes, did not attack me; I left the place after twelve o'clock, and the next day, without any accident, joined Colonel Donop at Crosswick.

Though all these rules be ever so excellent for the defence of a post, they will be of no effect, if the interior service of the garrison be not carried on with regularity and vigilance; and of course that sentries and guards are always watchful, and frequent rounds take place at uncertain hours; false alarms must be given, especially during the night, to try the alertness of officers and men, to fall in, each into his proper station: those who arrive first, must be publicly praised, and the late or slow, punished; besides the main and other guards, a piquet of a captain, two subalterns, and a hundred men must be always in readiness, as also an officer with fifty dragoons; the piquet officers must by turns visit the guards and sentries at different hours, for rounds made at certain fixed hours are of no service; the commander may however point out to the officers of the piquet the hours they must go their rounds, but this must not be known to the guards; he ought especially, during the night, to visit the posts himself, never depend entirely upon his inferiors, and be an example of alertness to the garrison.

Patroles must also be sent towards the enemy, more especially before daybreak; they must receive accurate orders where to go, and the commander of the *patrole* bring back a certificate of some of the principal inhabitants, to prove that they have really been there, observing that such *patroles* ought not to be always of the same number of men. For example: during the winter of 1761, in the seven years war, being an ensign in a detachment at Dryburg, under the command of a certain field officer of infantry, I recollect, that the *patroles* which went towards Stadtbergen were frequently carried off by the French, who occupied that place; a non-commissioned officer and fix dragoons were regularly sent every day, and an officer and 20 dragoons every third day, at a fixed hour: in spite of military etiquette, the lieutenant of the light dragoons once took the liberty to tell his commandant, if this method of patrolling was not changed, he would lose all his men one after the other; but the lieutenant-colonel, who was an older officer than the lieutenant, would not listen to his remonstrance; he answered, that it had been regulated in that manner by the field officer whom he had relieved; no alteration was made, and the French continued carrying off more *patroles*.

After sunset, the gates must be shut, and never be opened during night, without the commandant's permission; and even then, the guard must previously be turned out, and a reconnoitring party with an officer must descend the wall upon a ladder, which ought to be in readiness for that purpose; nor are the gates to be opened in the morning before the return of the *patroles* which have been sent out to ascertain that the enemy have not approached; in foggy weather they must always remain shut, as also when intelligence is received that the enemy be in motion; and in this case, the guards must be doubled, and frequent *patroles* sent towards the enemy, though he be at a great distance. For instance: during the expedition of January, 1761, the hereditary prince intended to carry Fritzlar by a *coup de main*; Captain Isedom, of the Prussian black hussars, who had the advance guard of the prince's corps, rushed by noon so near to the castle gate of Fritzlar, that the French had hardly time to shut the gate.

2ndly, during the attack of the Austrian army upon the Prussian corps of General Fink at Maxen, the former had occupied Dipholswalda: this post was very important, as it covered their rear, and the officer who commanded in it ought to have been particularly vigilant; but on the contrary, he suffered the duty to be carried on very negligently; for the Prussian Colonel Kleist, on his return from an inroad in Bohemia, entered the district of Dipholswalda, without General Seckendorf having the least information of it; the then Lieutenant Kumpel, supported by a captain and 100 men of Corbiere's battalion, which belonged to Colonel Kleist's corps, and a field piece, surprised with 50 men the Austrian guard of 100 at the gate, killed and took many prisoners, and entered the town with the fugitives.

In such important occurrences, the best plan would be to send always a small party with an officer or a non-commissioned officer after the usual *patroles*, and especially those which go out at daybreak; these parties must proceed slowly on the same road as the *patroles* in front, and frequently halt and listen; should they hear a firing, they must instantly communicate this or any other intelligence to the commandant, for if the *patroles* do their duty, they cannot be carried off by the enemy without a shot; but if everything appear quiet, the parties should halt about halfway, and wait for the return of the *patrole* in front, and the arrival of the cross *patrole*: supposing that the enemy have carried off the first *patrole*, the parties and cross *patroles* will at least discover and announce the approach of the enemy.

Had General Meyer used these precautions at his post of Weistritz, whilst the King of Prussia was besieging Olmutz, that truly great general would not have been surprised by General St. Ignon; for although he received intelligence from Field Marshal Keith about the movements of the Austrians, he remained in perfect security, seeing everything quiet before his post at daybreak, and having his *patroles* actually out towards the enemy, who in fact had carried them off.

If there be a post-office in the place, the post-master must be forbidden to deliver letters, or furnish any person with horses without your permission; an officer must besides be placed on duty in the house, to open all letters and send you such as may contain interesting intelligence. All travellers without exception, notwithstanding their passports, must be thoroughly examined; fairs and public amusements or ceremonies must be forbidden, for under that cover, many a post has been surprised.

In order to guard against surprisals, you must procure spies among the inhabitants, especially those who live near the enemy, they will give you early intelligence of his motions; you can also (particularly if you have reasons to suspect an attack) place at night some small posts around the place; the men on this duty must be acquainted with a certain signal which they are to make for procuring immediate admittance into the place, should they have intelligence to communicate in the night-time; for instance, they must strike their firelocks with the hand a certain number of strokes, or cough so many times, observing that those signals must be changed for every party that go out a scouting; the guards at the gates must also be very attentive to observe people going in and out, and stop such as appear suspicious, or strangers.

If the guards on the steeple perceive a number of waggons or troops at a distance, should they approach from any other side than that from which you might expect the enemy, and the colour of the clothing of the troops induce you to conclude that they be friends, the gates must however be instantly shut, and an officer sent out with a few men to reconnoitre; the officer must at a certain distance call out halt! and should the waggons be laden or covered, they must be carefully searched as well as the conductors, in order to ascertain that no men are concealed in the waggons, and that the conductors are unarmed; troops must also be ordered to halt at a distance, and the reconnoitring officer desire their commander to approach alone, and if he obey, conduct him into the town; should it be an enemy, the officer must order his men to fire, and make off as well as they can.

If you post or a neighbouring one have been alarmed by the enemy, be doubly on your guard. For instance, in the winter of 1777, when part of the English army under Lord Cornwallis was cantoned in and about New Brunswick, in the province of Jersey, the Americans for two days successively alarmed the posts of Ponentown and Piscataway, and on the third fell upon my post at daybreak, during a thick fog: the *patrole* which I had sent out before daybreak was already returned, and had perceived nothing; but as the fog began with the dawn, I sent another *patrole* out, and remained under arms: this *patrole* had hardly marched a hundred paces when they met the enemy, who was repulsed with loss, and pursued to his own quarters by the prompt assistance of Captain Wreeden and his company.

An exact compliance with these rules will render it almost impossible that the enemy should surprise you, or even approach unperceived; however, should you be attacked in a post which you are ordered to maintain, honour must be preferred to life, and the possession of the post dearly sold to the enemy: in such a circumstance, I advise the commanding officer to ask no advice from his inferiors, listen to no representation, and to persevere in the resolution he may have formed: a glorious death is certainly preferable to life at the price of ever so good a capitulation; thus in the campaign of 1758, the Prussian Colonel Meyer defended Marienberg in the Erzgeburge with his free corps, against 3000 Austrians; and with the same gallantry did the British Colonel Cruger defend, in 1781, the post of Ninety Six, in South Carolina, against 7000 Americans, commanded by general green, who was forced to retire with a severe loss, after an unsuccessful attempt.

Artifice may also compensate for inferiority of strength; extraordinary measures will frequently prove the best: for instance, after the Battle of Hochkirch, which gave the Austrians the whole of Saxony, excepting Dresden and Torgau, the Prussian Colonel Grohlman, with a garrison battalion and a small detachment of hussars, occupied Torgau; General Haddick, informed of the weakness of the garrison, attempted to carry the town; upon the approach of the enemy, Colonel Grohlman felt himself greatly embarrassed, having no other defence than a feeble entrenchment, which he had not even men enough to line sufficiently; he acquainted immediately with his situation General Wedel, who commanded the advance guard of Count Dohna's army, which had already advanced as far as Hertzberg on its march to the relief of Saxony; but Hertzberg being six leagues distant from Torgau, the latter might easily have been carried before any succour could have arrived: the Prussian colonel took his resolution instantly, unable to resist by force, he applied to artifice, and with 300 men and his hussars advanced as far as the large pond, towards General Haddick, who, acquainted with the march of Count Dohna's army, and struck by the boldness of the Prussians, concluded that General Wedel was already arrived at Torgau; he retreated accordingly, and Torgau was preserved: this example proves, that a truly great mind will find resources in the most desperate situation.

The position of the winter cantonments may also require that certain posts should be occupied, which are badly calculated for defence. For example, Gelnhausen, which is upon the route between Hanau and Fulda, is surrounded by a good wall with a kind of rampart walk on it, and from which you command an extensive view of part of the country towards the South, East, and West; only the northerly side is surrounded by mountains, from one of which called the Durich, the town, built as an amphitheatre at its foot, is commanded in such a manner, that from the top you can fire with small arms upon all the streets.

Supposing that the enemy's army have taken their quarters on the left bank of the Mayn, and occupy Frankfort, Aschaffenburg, and Hanau, the chain of the opponent army extend from Giesen to Butzbach, Friedberg, Assenheim, Ordenberg, and Budingen to Gelnhausen; in this case, Gelnhausen must be occupied, and in order to guard against insults from the enemy, (being on account of the rigour of the season obliged to put your men under cover) the only resource will be to erect upon the Durich a redoubt, garrisoned with a hundred men and two pieces of artillery; thus you may easily defend the place, as the Durich commands all the other mountains; there being plenty of wood in the neighbourhood, a guard-house may be built of whole trees, with a fireplace, to preserve the men from excessive cold: had Colonel Rall erected a redoubt for 200 men with the 6 field pieces of his three regiments upon the road of Maidenhead to Trentown, at the top of the height, from whence he could have commanded the whole place.

General Washington would never have attempted to attack him, as the success of the enterprise depended upon its being performed expeditiously: but the brave Colonel Rall was deaf to the repeated intelligence he received of the design of the enemy, who being aware of this, seized the opportunity, and succeeded. If a post must be occupied, though incapable of defence, the commanding officer should consider his safety as depending entirely upon spies, frequent *patroles*, and uncommon vigilance; should the enemy approach with a superior force, he will be enabled to withdraw at a moment's notice, for the intention of the enemy is obviously to carry the garrison, and not to occupy a bad post himself.

For example, during the winter quarters of 1760, General Luckner with 3000 men, chiefly light troops, was sent to Heiligenstadt, in order to cover the left flank of Duke Ferdinand's quarters, and to secure the communication with the Prussian army; this town is so completely surrounded with mountains, that every issue is a long *defilé*; the Duke of Broglies resolved to carry the post, and appointed for that expedition part of the garrison of Göttingen, and some of the troops upon the Werra; the French observed such a secrecy on their march, that General Luckner was not aware of it until the morning of the 23rd of December, and when he saw them, he was already cut off from

Nordheim, Duderstadt, and Lindau; having no retreat left but upon Witzenhausen, he resolved to take this road, though it led towards the enemy's quarters, and was so fortunate in his escape, that he lost only 34 men, who were slow in quitting the town; he took a position near the place upon a height about the Sharfenstein, from whence his artillery fired upon the French, who did not pursue him, and he retired upon Worbis.

Section 4
Of Reconnoitring

Reconnoitring the enemy is one of the most difficult duties in war. The motives for reconnoitring are various, A partisan is often sent out to examine a strong place or post, or the access of the enemy's camp; or the general may wish to reconnoitre such himself, and takes with him thence a partisan, as an escort, expecting that he has already some knowledge of the country. This duty requires great skill, and particularly a keen eye.

If you have to reconnoitre in open countries, the detachment which is employed should consist of cavalry, supported by infantry.

Should the country be so hilly and intersected that you cannot approach the enemy with cavalry, infantry must be employed, and the cavalry posted behind them in the open places, in order, that should the infantry be pressed upon by the enemy, they may be ready to support them. The main point is, in such a case, not to advance to the enemy with the whole detachment at once, but divide it into two, three, four, or even fix parties, one of which may support the other: you ought to regulate your measures according to the nature of the ground, and the length of your march. As you approach the enemy, every *defilé* or cross road which you leave behind, and which you are not perfectly acquainted with, mud be occupied.

Thus, if you be repulsed by the enemy, you fall back from one detachment to another whereby the enemy in his pursuit will be embarrassed, finding that your force encreases every step which you retreat. As you can seldom go farther when reconnoitring an enemy's piquet, than to drive back his outposts, you require only so many men as are necessary to support the reconnoitring party. In order to arrive in front of the enemy's outposts at daybreak, much is not hazarded in such cases, if you observe secrecy on your march; for before the outpost are driven back, and other detachments arrive, you may have completed your intentions: but as the enemy will also employ every means to hinder you from approaching too near, and will fall upon you with force as soon as he perceives you, it is well to observe the before-mentioned rule, and divide your detachment into two, three, four, or six parties, leaving them at certain distances from each other, and approach the enemy only with one, in order to have a resource: with one of these parties attack the enemy's outposts resolutely, drive them back, make your observations, and retire back again as quick as possible. You must not spare yourself, but advance as near as possible to the object which you wish to examine, by which means much may be seen in war,

I always followed this rule in the American war, and never confined my reconnoitring to the worded orders, to accomplish to the utmost what was entrusted to me; but I always went farther, in order to see or do nothing by halves, by which I often experienced, how much a man may perform who takes a pleasure in his duty: for the officer, who will only do that in war which he is ordered, and will hazard no more, especially when leading a light corps, does scarcely any thing, and can by no means be reckoned an useful officer.

Inasmuch as the art of reconnoitring requires skill, toil, and precaution, when occasion requires you to force your way, so the like skill, as good an eye, and as much toil are required from those who are sent out to reconnoitre certain roads, passes, and rivers. In these cases, you must go as far as you can, and observe everything accurately. For instance: whether cavalry, artillery and baggage can come along the road easily, or with difficulty; whether the ground be hard or swampy; if the road lead through much wood, how broad it is, how many *defilés* you meet with, and on which side they are commanded; how wide the rivers are, whether their banks be high, if grown over with bushes, and which bank is the highest; how many fords in the neighbourhood, and how deep, whether the ground and bottom be hard or muddy, how many bridges, whether of stone or wood, and how broad. You must not for this depend upon the intelligence of one or two inhabitants in the neighbourhood, but question many; nor ask them whether you can pass, but only signify that you must pass, be the consequence what it may.

Nor must you question the rich inhabitants, for they will always represent the roads worse than they really are, in order to prevent a visit into their country: you must examine yourself, by which you can give a satisfactory report, and not expose yourself to be found inaccurate. For I have experienced in the American war, when the inhabitants of the country have described roads as very bad, which have been found upon trial equal to the best high roads.

In order to render this rule more clear, I will here give an example, respecting the reconnoitring of a strong post. Supposing, that I was sent with a corps from Gelnhausen to protect an engineer, who is ordered to reconnoitre the fortifications of Hanau. As it is very advantageous, especially when reconnoitring fortified places, to take prisoners, in order to get intelligence of the garrison, and the interior situation of the fortress, it must however be done by the reconnoitring party with as much circumspection as haste.

The corps consists of two companies of riflemen of 450, two light infantry companies of the same number, and two squadrons of light cavalry of 456, Supposing it to be the season, when the day begins to dawn about five, and night begins about eight o'clock; the road is five long leagues; we will set off from Gelnhausen at ten o'clock at night; 100 cavalry and 100 riflemen, conducted by an able officer, march to Meerholz, Neuhaslau, and Rodenbach.

This detachment, as soon as it has passed Neuhaslau, sends an officer with 10 riflemen and 10 cavalry to occupy Röckinger bridge, and some riflemen steal into the village and get intelligence when the last *patroles* of the enemy were there, how strong they are in general, and how often they come from Hanau; all of which the officer reports to his commander. As soon as this detachment is arrived at the issue of Rodenbach's Wood, 50 cavalry, and as many riflemen, remain here, in order to secure the retreat of those who go towards Hanau. The commander of the latter approaches hereupon with 40 cavalry, and as many riflemen, through Bulau, as near the fortress as possible, sends a scouting *patrole* towards Lehnhof, and endeavours to get intelligence of the enemy. As soon as it is day, he shews himself, in order to draw the attention of the town upon that side: if the enemy have occupied the Lambois bridge, he endeavours to surprise the enemy's piquet, or to disperse them. He sends some trusty *yägers* as near to the wall as possible, to fire upon the sentries, or whatever may appear.

As the reconnoitring party must take place on the right bank of the Kintzig, the commander of the corps, together with the engineer, takes his march over Langenselbold; a company of light infantry remain here behind, who place themselves in the gardens, which lie upon a height towards Ruckingen; 200 cavalry remain at Ruckingen, and the second company of light infantry remain in the coppice of Ruckingen. The commander of the corps sends three or four small parties into this country, each of which must consist of only four or fix well mounted and trusty cavalry, who will advance to Neuhof, Kintzingerhof, Fisherhof, the Fasanerie, and Williamsbad, in order to take any of the soldiers or officers of the garrison prisoners, who certainly will be upon these heights over night.

The commander of the whole takes then the remaining rifle company, together with the remaining 156 cavalry, and approaches the town under cover of the night, through the Gehegewald, as near as possible, in order that the engineer can begin his reconnoitring at daybreak. As everything that comes out of the town must come through the Mühlschanzenthor, or over the Kintz bridge, in front of the suburbs, it is only necessary to keep a good eye upon these two issues. Should the enemy come out of the town with his cavalry, or a great part of his garrison, the two detachments having much wood behind them, have little to fear. The detachment which approached the town through the Bulau, can retreat from wood to wood, as far as Altenhasslau.

The detachment, which advanced over Ruckingen, retires from post to post; and as it will be thrice reinforced, on a road of only two small leagues, the enemy will hardly hazard much, but be content, by the assurance, that the detachment not being able to ascertain the object, has retreated again. If he press too closely upon one of the two detachments, he must also hazard being taken in the rear by the other; and as both detachments have a communication with each other by the different bridges, which are between Langelselbold and Hanau, over the Kintzing, he may be completely cut off from Hanau.

The method of reconnoitring, which I have here proposed for instruction, may be also employed usefully against posts and camps; nothing is hazarded by it, whilst the rear is covered in the neighbourhood and at a farther distance, and the retreat safe.

SECTION 5
OF SURPRISALS.

The word surprisal, properly speaking, should not be known in war; and if an officer would only consider the offensive meaning attached to it, such occurrences would very seldom, if ever, happen. For to say an officer has been surprised, is the same as saying he has lost by his own negligence, ignorance, or obstinacy the honour, liberty, or lives of himself and many men who were entrusted to him; and can an officer, who has caused this misfortune by his own fault, be more injured in the opinion of the world than when he be so spoken of? Notwithstanding the great care which an officer is forced to take in the execution of his trust when on a post in the field, yet we find instances of this kind in every war; for he who hazards a surprisal will seldom fail; and those surprisals, which are looked upon as impossible by the common run of men, turn out in general the most successful.

Though surprisals require so much prudence, skill, expedition and secrecy in the execution, yet they are so far useful in war, not only for the actual advantage, but because they depress the enemy: if you will hazard such an attempt upon the enemy, the principal point is to have an accurate knowledge of the country. You must have good spies and guides; the first are necessary to procure intelligence of the enemy's strength, how his posts are situated, and in what manner, whether the duty be carried on negligently, where and how far his *patroles* go, how strong, how often they go out, how far the next post is distant from that which you intend to surprise, what kind of a man the commander is, whether he be of an easy temper, or addicted to dissipation. The guides are necessary, in order to conduct you by by-ways to the enemy, and shew you accurately every access by which you can cut off the enemy, and completely surround him.

For if such enterprises only half succeed, or wholly miscarry, you make yourself ridiculous in the eyes of the enemy, and lose the confidence of your men. For instance; in the surprise of Baumbridge in the spring of 1777, the English cavalry had crossed the River Rariton, a quarter of a league above the place where they ought to have done so, in order to cut off the Americans from the pass, which was the reason that General Lincoln himself, and instead of 200, 800 men were not taken prisoners. The same fault was committed in the surprise of the corps under the Marquis de la Fayette in the spring of 1778, near Germantown. In successful or unsuccessful expeditions, it is necessary to be acquainted with more than one road, that you may retire by the shortest. Night is the best time for such *coups de main*, it spreads terror among the enemy when he finds himself attacked on all sides; he cannot discover the motions, he cannot distinguish the true from the false attack, he beholds everything double through fear, and trees and hedges will at this time be taken for men. I have once been an eye-witness of a false alarm. One can hardly conceive how much fear works upon men just roused from sleep.

It was in the campaign of Pennsylvania when General Howe wished to cross the Chulkhill after the Battle of Brandywine River; the Hessian and Anspachs' *yäger* corps stood in a wood not far from French Creek; they had the rear, and lay ready with their arms to march on the first signal. A few shots were fired by the piquets, which gave occasion to the inhabitants of a neighbouring plantation to scream out aloud; at once, a voice cried out "run, we are surprised!" The whole corps dispersed in every direction; a whole hour was employed to reassemble the men, and they could hardly be convinced that all this had been only a false alarm.

A mist, a strong wind with rain, or a fall of snow, are the opportunities which may contribute to your success in a surprise, for *patroles* are seldom found upon the roads in very bad weather, as one may suppose that it may hinder the enemy from approaching. A thick mist will favour your approach; and when hard rain and high wind drive in the faces of the sentries, they put down their heads, forget themselves often, and turn their backs to the rain and wind, by which you may easily steal to them, and stab them unawares. I know that I have often come to the most dangerous posts, where the sentries must have known that death or hard captivity would be the punishment for the least negligence, and have approached so near a sentry, that I have stood close to his front without being discovered. In such weather you cannot visit your own posts too often.

If you receive intelligence that a detachment of the enemy are about to take a certain post in the neighbourhood, or you believe from his situation that he will and must occupy a post, gain his rear, and as soon as it is night fall upon him. In this case you may, if the country be much intersected, ruin whole regiments with a handful of men. In this manner a French partisan, with 150 light infantry of Soubise's corps, surprised in the seven years war near Werle, four squadrons of hussars and a battalion of light infantry of the allied army. It was in August in the campaign of 1761. The then hereditary prince, now Duke of Brunswick, stood between Hamm and Werle, near Bockum, which place lay in front of the prince's left wing.

Two leagues in front of the prince lay Werle, a town surrounded by a dry ditch, and a wall; the French had occupied Lüne and the castle of Kappenberg, and were patrolling Werle. The Prince of Brunswick detached a colonel of hussars with his regiment, and a battalion of light infantry to Werle, in order to observe the French in and near Lüne. The commander of this corps took post close to the town, placed his outposts immediately on his arrival, which commanded the road towards Lüne and Kappenberg, and sent out proper *patroles*; the hussars kept saddled in the daytime, and bridled in the night; the free battalion stood so near the town that they placed their arms against the wall, but notwithstanding all this precaution, the detachment was surprised the first night: the French officer, who commanded in Lüne, as soon as he heard that Werle was about to be occupied, took 150 men, marched over Kappenberg, and placed himself between Bockum and Werle in the wood, where he waited until night.

A heavy storm began about midnight, by favour of which he approached the enemy as near as possible. He divided his detachment in two parties, one of which was to attack the hussars, the other the light infantry. Having fired, he rushed with charged bayonets upon the battalion, killed many, carried off what he could, and retreated the shortest way from Werle to Lüne: as soon as the prince received this intelligence, he pursued the French with some cavalry, but they had too short a journey, and were not to be overtaken.

In the same manner an American party was surprised at mid-day, not far from Gloucester Church in Virginia. Colonel Simcoe, who was ordered to cover a foraging party in this country, received intelligence from a Negro, just as the foraging was completed, that an American detachment had come to Ward's Plantation, a league and half from the abovementioned church; and the Negro added, that he had not perceived that they had placed any outposts. Hereupon the colonel took 100 cavalry, in order to fall upon the enemy before he had time to collect himself, and ordered me to follow him with the *yägers* and his light infantry as quick as possible. We found everything as the Negro had informed us; but to the enemy's good luck, and our disappointment, two American dragoons were marauding, who discovered the colonel with, his cavalry, galloped back, and gave an alarm, whereupon all fled into the neighbouring thicket, and thus we could only take an officer, five horses, and seven men. But as their horses were not saddled, and they had not time to take away their arms, we ordered the saddles to be burnt, and the arms to be broken to pieces.

The first example proves, that one ought never to occupy a post before the whole country is thoroughly searched, to be assured that no party of the enemy lay concealed in the neighbourhood. One should also always secure the rear, and endeavour to preserve a communication with the corps which is behind; for the officer at Werle could have avoided in two different ways the misfortune which befell him, and the chagrin which he must have felt for ever after. As Werle as surrounded with a wall, and is calculated for defence, he might have gone with his whole detachment into this place, and have observed the enemy by the detachments which he should have sent to Lüne and Kappenberg, and have kept open a communication with the prince by *patroles*; or otherwise he might have sought out an advantageous post near the town for half of his detachment, and have placed the other half between his post and Bockum, in order by this means to have covered his rear; or he might have sent his hussars before, and have so posted the battalion of light infantry, that his rear would have been covered.

The last example shews, that an officer should not remain from his post a moment, without taking proper measures for his safety. For had not Fortune favoured the American officer, his whole detachment would have been lost.

You may also surprise the enemy, if you can approach near him undiscovered. In this case his outposts should be rushed upon, and endeavour to enter his camp at the same time with him. As, however, such enterprises should be undertaken with the greatest expedition, only cavalry can be employed, unless the country be so intersected by wood and hills, that only light infantry can be used. In the campaign of South Carolina in 1780, Colonel Tarleton with 200 cavalry surprised at mid-day 2000 Americans under General Sumpter. The English rushed upon the Americans with such fury that the latter had not time to take up their arms, which they had piled together before their huts. Had Colonel Armand when he surprised the *yäger* piquet at mid-day, near Courtland's Plantation, in the province of New York, gone through the ravine which separated the corps from the mountain, upon which the right wing of the piquet was posted, he might have retaliated upon the *yäger* corps in the same manner, for before we had perceived the event in the camp he might have been in the middle of us.

One may also keep the enemy in constant alarm in order to lull him into a false security, and then at once fall upon him. This generally succeeds best about noon, because the enemy considers himself as most secure at this time, and those who have watched the preceding night are at rest. The horses are fed at that hour, the officers consider more their conveniency, some are at dinner, and amongst those corps, where the severest discipline is not practised, many may be found either out of the camp feasting with their friends, or in the neighbouring villages. I know, that in many different English corps two officers were seldom to be found in camp at noon hour. The American partisans Otterndorf and Butler chose this time two days running during the winter cantonments at Brunswick, in order to surprise me; but they were received contrary to their expectations, and driven back from both attempts.

If on the march to the enemy there be a *defilé* or a river to pass, or you leave a bridge behind you, and you are forced to return by it, occupy such a pass with light infantry, to secure you from not being cut off on a retreat. For instance, supposing you would surprise the enemy in the country of Hanau, near Seligenstadt or Babenhausen, and cross on your march the Mayn near Steinheim or Rumpenheim, you must occupy the castle of Steinheim, or in the other the nearest gardens and houses of Rumpenheim. Or, supposing you would surprise the enemy from Windecken, in or near Friedberg, you must occupy the bridge over the Wetter, near the convent of Ilbenstadt. Light infantry may also surprise cavalry when quartered in open places as well as in intersected countries. In the first instance, you steal at night time as near the enemy as possible, and fire a volley, whereby the horses will certainly start and prevent the riders from mounting.

Upon this fall immediately upon the enemy, kill, or take prisoners, as many as you can, and retreat as quick as possible. In the last instance, if you can steal secretly into the cavalry's cantonments, divide your detachment into different parties, one-half of which must endeavour to make themselves master of the stables, whilst the others seize the men. For example, in the American war, in 1776, Count Pulawsky quartered in one of the plantations near Eckharbour, in the province of New Jersey, in order to cover this country against the landing and pillage of the English privateers, Major Ferguson, one of the most meritorious and bravest officers of the English army, crossed from Long Island with a party of Scots, landed at Eckharbour in the night-time in the rear of Pulawsky's quarters, killed all the horses and many men, and took the greatest part of the latter prisoners along with him.

You must never forget in surprises to cover the side, whence the enemy can come to assist the post which you intend to surprise.

With respect to what is to be observed on the march, I refer the reader to the chapter in which I have treated on secret marches. I will now particularly observe that in this instance, as the march is undertaken generally in the night, no flankers can be employed. The advance guard is to be quite near, before which an officer goes on foot at the distance of 50 paces, who must often stand still, and should he discover any men at a distance, must report it immediately. Should they be an enemy's *patrole*, you must halt in order not to be discovered, and endeavour to take them. Should you, however; be already discovered, you must give up your intentions immediately; everyone should march in the greatest silence, smoak no tobacco, and all those who are subject to coughs and colds must be left behind on such occasion. No horse must be taken that is accustomed to neigh.

The following surprisal, which is one of the most remarkable in the seven years war, will make the before-mentioned rules more clear to the reader, especially if he will take Rosier's map of Hessia before him. It was when the Hereditary Prince of Brunswick surprised the French corps under General Claubiz, near Emsdorf in Upper Hessia,

In the campaign of 1760 the allied army were placed upon the heights of Sachsenhausen, and the French, under the Marshal de Broglio, near Corbach. The Prince of Brunswick was detached with a corps, in order to defeat the French corps under General Claubiz, who had advanced beyond Neustadt to the heights of Wasenberg in order to cut off the communication between the fortress of Ziegenhayn and the allied army. The prince, therefore, went off on the 14th of July at evening from Sachsenhausen to Fritzlar, to which place six battalions of the army had already marched.

These proceeded on the 15th to Zwesten, where General Luckner joined them with his hussars and Elliot's light dragoons, and continued the march towards Treifa, where they received intelligence that the enemy had proceeded from Wasenberg to Emsdorf, upon which the prince ordered his corps to rest at Treifa. On the 16th he had advanced as far as Speckswinkel, where Major Frederick and Colonel Frytag had followed the enemy with his *yägers* in order to observe him. The prince here reconnoitred the situation of the enemy, and found that he had encamped advantageously, as Emsdorf lay in front of his right wing, and a wood covered his left.

Hereupon the prince marched off with five battalions and the *yägers* through the wood upon Wolferode, in order to fall upon the enemy's rear and left flank, during which General Luckner with his cavalry and an Hanoverian battalion, which the prince had ordered to remain in a valley behind Speckswinkel, was to fall on the enemy's right wing, where the French cavalry stood. Both attacks succeeded, and the enemy, who had not received the least intelligence of the prince's march, was surprised in his camp at mid-day. All that could get under arms endeavoured to make some resistance in order to save the honour of the whole; but they were in too great disorder to avoid, by any means, the unfortunate consequences. They therefore took flight through a thicket to Laogenstein, to which place the Hanoverian battalion of Baer pursued them; and whilst the routed enemy turned off from the village to a neighbouring thicket, the battalion went through the village and cut them off from the stone bridge over the Ohm, at the same time that a part of the cavalry cut off the pass to Amoeneburg.

The prince, not satisfied with this advantage, pursued the part of the enemy who endeavoured to save themselves towards Schweinsberg, came up with them in and near Niederklein, where they attempted again to make a defence, but finally shared the fate of the others. As well ordered and conduced as this *coup de main* was, yet it would have been impossible to have succeeded in it, had the enemy often patrolled, covered his rear, and not have been too sure of safety. For, had he posted one of his three infantry regiments in or near Kirchhayn, his retreat would have been secure over the Wehr and Ohm.

This proves how much judgement, skill and courage are necessary in surprises in the field. Moreover, those which are undertaken against inclosed or fortified posts are liable to far greater difficulties. In such cases you have to pass ditches, to climb walls and ramparts, and to force open gates; you will often meet with unforeseen obstacles, which must be removed before you can attain your object; notwithstanding by the negligence and want of dexterity of the enemy, and by money, a partisan has opportunities to provide for the success of the surprisal of a strong post.

For example, you may by your spies and the enemy's deserters be informed whether he be negligent in his duty, and do not attend to it with proper vigilance and precaution. You may be informed by an inhabitant, and shewn the access to a post which the enemy has not sufficiently occupied. You may have intelligence that the garrison of a post is too weak to occupy it with advantage. In a word, if an officer be not avaricious, he will always find traitors or friends for ready cash. This never failed with me in America when I wished to know whether this or that inhabitant of a plantation was a king's friend or a rebel; and I well know, that for money servants have even betrayed their own masters.

It is of no consequence what means you pursue for the success of surprises; but they require trusty spies and guides, who will give the best information, and lead you by the safest and most covered countries to the post or village. If the place be surrounded by dry ditches, with walls or ramparts, it is necessary to know the depth of the ditches, and the height of the ramparts, in order to regulate the size of the ladders accordingly, if you wish to escalade. The spies and guides must be acquainted with the town perfectly. They must know the main-guard, the alarm posts, and the strength of each guard, where the cavalry and infantry have their quarters, and where the head officers live. The farther you are from the enemy, the success of an undertaking is frequently the more certain, and the stronger a post is, the more remiss and negligent the garrison will probably be.

For example: Colonel Donop. was detached from Philadelphia, to carry the intrenched post of Redbank, and to cut off the communication of the garrison of Mud Island and the province of New Jersey, which was always furnished with provisions from the latter province. On the 20th of October in the morning, he crossed the Delaware not far from the town, marched to Hattenfield, where he remained the night; and though the march had not been held secret, we arrived on the 21st, at noon, so unexpectedly, in the neighbourhood of the enemy's posts, that we found a quartermaster with six soldiers a small quarter league from it, who were fetching meat from a neighbouring plantation for the garrison, and who assured us, that the enemy had not the least idea of our approach.

Had this moment been well employed, and we had fallen immediately on our arrival upon both sides of this post, as we could have approached by the help of a wood on the side of Philadelphia within 400 paces of it, we should certainly have surprised the enemy, and by which the lives of many brave officers and soldiers would have been spared, which were lost in the storm that took place in the afternoon at four o'clock, after we had summoned the enemy. For our summons was in fact nothing more than a warning to him to prepare for our attack.

Surprisals frequently succeed, when an army retreats after a check. In general, the opponent becomes elated by his success, and begins to look upon his enemy with contempt. The before-mentioned surprisals of Trainton, Prinztown, and Stony Point, were nothing more than the natural consequences of a contempt for the enemy. The negligence which had crept into the French army, in the Hanoverian campaign, when the allies under Duke Ferdinand drove them out of the Hanoverian territory, arose from the same cause, by which they were surprised almost in every post.

I will here give an instructive example from this campaign: as Count Chabot was at Hoya, and received the intelligence of the approach of the allied army, he thought it impossible that an enemy's corps could cross the Aller and Weser, as both rivers were very much overflowed; but he was mistaken, and was not well acquainted with his opponent, whose uncommon activity knew how to remove every obstacle. The Hereditary Prince of Brunswick carried on this enterprise against Hoya, in spite of every difficulty. For though he found only one ferry-boat, and some fishing boats, to cross the Weser near Barmen; and though a very heavy storm arose at the time when he had hardly transported half of his corps, by which the passage of the remaining troops was rendered wholly impossible, yet he was not discouraged from his undertaking, but continued his route with a handful of troops towards Hoya, where he arrived at six o'clock in the evening.

After the prince had taken every proper measure for an attack, he ordered no shot to be fired, but all were to charge with bayonets. But near Wülzen the advanced guard met with an enemy's *patrole*, upon which some of his men fired, and thereby the approach of the prince was discovered by the French. He was not, however, depressed by this accident, but rushed into the place. Meanwhile a part of the garrison collected in the streets, and defended themselves bravely; another part fired from the houses: Count Chabot endeavoured, as much as possible, to defend the bridge which led to the castle, but he was driven away from it; and had not the French set fire to some houses in this part of the town, the count would certainly have been cut off from the castle, or the allies would have entered it *pêle mêle* with them.

At daybreak the count was summoned in the castle. Seeing himself surrounded on every side, he requested a free retreat, which he obtained, from the particular generosity of this great prince. This example proves, how easily the best formed plan may be frustrated; for had not the soldiers of the allies advance-guard fired upon the enemy's *patrole*, the French would certainly have been surprised. In a surprisal, it is therefore best not to suffer the arms of the advance guard to be loaded, and particularly so in the night-time, in order to deprive the soldiers of every opportunity of firing. The prince took this method at Zierenberg, in Hessia, Which post was surprised in sight of the French army. The circumstance is too instructive, to be omitted.

In the campaign of 1760, when the allies and the French army were separated by the Dimel, the hereditary Prince of Brunswick crossed the river near Marburg, in the night of the 5th of September, and surprised this town at daybreak in the sight of the French army, Marburg covered the left flank of the army, and was occupied by the volunteers of Clermont and Dauphine, under Brigadier Nordmann,

As this enterprise required the utmost silence, the prince, to prevent any firing, would not suffer the arms to be loaded, for the French reserve, under General de Muy, stood only half a league beyond the town. A detachment of cavalry was posted between the enemy's army and Zierenberg, in order to cover the prince's enterprise on that side, and one of light infantry was sent in the country of Lahr, in order to secure the prince against the Stainville corps. Major Bülow placed himself between Zierenberg and Dürrenberg, in order to wholly cut off the enemy's retreat, and seize the fugitives. More than 300 men were killed; and Brigadier Nordmann, Colonel Comeras, 37 officers, and 417 men taken prisoners.

We will now take notice of those places, situated upon a river, where there are canals, or where water mills have a communication with the walls. For instance: Gelnhausen and Babenhausen, lying in the Wetterhau, may, by having intelligence with the inhabitants, be very easily surprised. A surprisal may also be undertaken, when you know that the enemy has bespoken workmen and forage in the neighbouring country. In the first case, a number of officers and soldiers must be dressed as peasants, each armed with a sword and pistol concealed under their clothes, and who must endeavour to approach without any noise so near the place, that at daybreak they may be near the gates. They should lay themselves down on both sides of the road, and wait the moment, when the gates are opened, rush upon the guards, and seize their arms.

Upon this they must endeavour to take post over the gates, and maintain it until the troops, which have been concealed in the neighbourhood for a support, arrive. In the second case, drive a number of waggons, so laden with straw or hay, that four or five men can conceal themselves in each under the forage; two or three disguised soldiers go with each waggon, and one with every two horses. At a certain distance from the enemy's post, a corps of cavalry lie concealed in a thicket, or behind a height, who, if the scheme succeeds, can hasten for a support. The waggons approach the post, and should the enemy be imprudent enough to open the gates, without searching, the first is driven under the gates, to prevent their being shut again suddenly.

The moment they think themselves matters of the gates, the disguised men fall upon the guards, seize them, and endeavour to maintain their post, until the neighbouring concealed support can gallop up to them. Little or nothing is hazarded by such enterprises; for supposing the enemy discovers the plot at the beginning, his whole attention will be employed to shut and defend the gates, which will give sufficient time for the party to retire.

In the night time, you can also advance with a detachment of cavalry to the enemy's post, on full gallop, and give yourselves out at the gates for one of his own detachments, which is routed and pursued by the enemy. You eagerly request admittance from the guards, telling them, that on the contrary, you must fall into the hands of the enemy who are pursuing. For instance: in the beginning of the year 1632, Duke Bernhard Von Weymar surprised Manheim in this manner: he took 500 Swedish cavalry, who galloped to the gates at midnight. They gave themselves out for an imperial regiment, who were routed in the neighbourhood by the Swedes, and were pursued.

Upon this pressing representation, the officer on duty ordered the gates to be opened. As soon as the Swedes came up to the guards, they cut them down. The garrison, awakened by the firing and noise, attempted to hasten to their rendezvous, but as the Swedes had already spread themselves in parties in every street, they were cut down one after the other as they arrived. Meanwhile, however, a part of the garrison had collected and prepared for a defence: but Duke Von Weymar now arrived with a part of his infantry, got over the walls, and ordered the men to advance on all sides, by which, in a short time, he was matter of the whole town. Count Maravalla, a Spanish general, who commanded the garrison, being exchanged, was publicly beheaded at Heidelberg.

It is also easy to surprise an enemy's post, if acquainted with some of the principal inhabitants of the place, and you know that the commander is fond of pleasure. In this case, make an appointment with one of your friends, to invite a large party on such a day, at your own expense, in which he must promote dancing and hard drinking, during which you make your attempt.

The great Elector, Frederic William, surprised in this manner the Swedes at Rhatenau, in the war of 1675. He sallied out of Franconia with his army, and hastened to the assistance of his hereditary possessions, which were in the hands of the Swedes: but in order to conceal his approach from the enemy, he ordered, as soon as he arrived at Magdeburg, the gates to be shut and made fast, and detached General Doerfling to surprise Rhatenau. The general, an hour before daybreak, arrived, undiscovered, in front of the town; gave himself out for a Swedish party, who had been routed by the Brandenburgians, and being pursued by them, requested admittance. This being granted immediately, he cut down the guards, and took possession of the town. The Swedish officers having been liberally entertained the preceding evening by a nobleman of the town, (which entertainment had been previously concerted by him and the Elector) had no sooner awoke in the morning, than they were either killed, or taken prisoners. with their soldiers.

The enemy may also be surprised in open day, by disguise. For instance: the hereditary Prince of Brunswick, in the surprisal of the French corps near Emsdorf, ordered the Hanoverians and Hessians to lay aside their coats. As these men now appeared white at a distance, the French guards took them for troops of their army, and suffered them to approach too near, which well thought of scheme contributed in a great measure to the fortunate success which was the consequence.

I will conclude the section with an example, which will very much illustrate the foregoing rules, since it was performed on the theatre of the seven years war, and of which very good charts are to be found. Take the map of the Wetterau. Supposing Hanau and Seeligenstadt already in our possession. I am at Aschaffenburg with a corps. The enemy is master of Fuldaschen and the Wetterau, and has extended his cordon from Saalmünster, over Bierstein, Budingen, Ortenburg, Staaten, Friedberg, &c. &c, Gelnhausen is not yet occupied by the enemy, but expecting, as it covers the entrance into the mountains, that he will occupy it afterwards, I have engaged a miller, to inform me, as soon as the enemy have occupied this town, and to procure me two or three trusty citizens of Gelnhausen, which will not be attended with much difficulty, as the greatest part of the inhabitants consist of Braconniers.[1]

As the success of my attempt must depend upon the negligence of the enemy, we will suppose, that he has not occupied the mill of the before-mentioned millers, which stands close to the walls, and through which they may be gained. The enemy have not also observed, that the Kintzing can be crossed above the lord of the manor's gardens, (where this river is divided by an island) and also near the mill. The enemy's detachment consists of 1000 infantry and 400 cavalry. In order to surprise him, I take 800 infantry, and 400 cavalry: supposing farther, that the campaign is nearly finished, and the season when it is equal day and night, at fun set the gates of Aschaffenburg

---

1. Men who live by killing game, in defiance of law, and even armed forces.

are shut, everyone is allowed to come in the town—but for 48 hours no one is permitted to go out.

The gates being shut, the detachment is ordered to go out, and is provided with bread and oats for two days. But as Aschaffenburg is ten leagues from Gelnhausen, the roads over the Spessart not the best, and the country very mountainous, this march cannot be made in one night, without tiring the men too much. I march therefore the first night as far as the country of Irbach and Köningshof, in Kahlgrund, where I am only four leagues distant from Gelnhausen. In this country I remain somewhat concealed, taking care to have water near, which, in a resting place upon a secret march, should be always considered, I remain here till the following night, and for security, place small guards around me, under trusty non-commissioned officers, at the distance of about 500 or 600 paces: these guards must keep concealed, and seize all those who pass, and not release them until the enterprise be completed.

As soon as night begins, I proceed, regulating my march in such a manner, that I arrive at midnight between the Eichhof and Eiden-Gesäsz, where I prepare for the attack, and divide the detachment as follows: 100 cavalry, and as many infantry, go off with a trusty guide. This detachment leaves Altenhaszlau on the right; crosses the Kintzing by the Kintzing Mill, leaves there for its security a non-commissioned officer and 10 *yägers*, in order to cover the bridge, and protect the miller and his family; takes its route over Rhode, occupies the heights, over which the road leads to Budingen, and so posts itself, that nothing can come upon it unawares from that side. Should this detachment be closely pressed by the enemy, it retires over the Kintzing to the mill, defends this post till further orders, and, if the surprisal succeeds, he returns in this case the same way, in order to join again the whole near Meerholz.

A captain with 100 infantry follows the first across the Kintzing, then leaves the village of Rhode on the left, and proceeds through the vineyards to Dürich, observes the road, which here leads through the Kohlgrund to Bierstein and Budingen, and cuts off the fugitives who attempt to save themselves through the Holzthor. This detachment must make its retreat, as soon as it hears any firing towards Budingen or Bierstein, to the Kintzing mill, and join the former.

A captain with 100 infantry, with a trusty guide, takes his route towards Höchst, passes the bridge over the Kintzing, approaches the Heitzer-gate, posts himself in the vineyards, in order to cut off the retreat of the enemy to Bierstein, and observes at the same time the roads leading to this town. Should the enemy receive succour from that side; this detachment retires round the town to the Holzthor, and takes the same road as the former. But as soon as it hears any firing towards Budingen, it must immediately think about its retreat, for if it cannot take the road to the Höchster bridge, it is cut off. 50 cavalry and 100 infantry remain upon the height as a reserve behind Altenhaszlau. The commander of this detachment endeavours to lay together a great heap of wood and wet straw, in order, at an appointed time, to make a fire, which may give a great smoke, and serve the detachment, that is towards Budingen, as a signal for a retreat. All prisoners should also be brought to it. The remaining 400 infantry I divide into 16 divisions, and the 250 cavalry into 10.

As soon as I suppose that each detachment may be arrived at its post, I take the straight road to the lord of the manor's garden, where the cavalry in the greatest silence, form up on the road that leads to Burgthor. With the infantry I cross the Kintzing to the mill, observing the deepest silence during the passage, which must be effected in close column of divisions, and the men forbidden, under pain of death, to quit their division, assuring them in the mean time that the booty will be equally divided, but those who go out for plunder shall lose their share, and be severely punished.

When the two first divisions have passed the mill, they steal to the Zügel-gates, surprise the guards, open the gates, pass the bridge, surprise the guards at Zügel-haus, open the Zügel-hausthor, observing to send information of it to the cavalry, who then gallop into the town, leaving behind them fifty men upon their post:, in order to seize the fugitives that run out of the castle. Two divisions hasten to the Schiffthor and to the Roderthor, in order to make themselves masters of them, and thereby hinder any part of the garrison from fleeing on that side. The twelve remaining divisions pass the Schimdtgasse to the lower market, one of which is ordered to search out the principal officers and seize them. Two hasten to the upper market, to force the Grand Guard. The remainder disperse in small parties through every street, and the cavalry that are already in the town, do the fame. These latter must now endeavour as much as possible, to hinder the enemy from collecting, kill or destroy all that oppose them, and not think of taking prisoners until they find they are in complete possession of the town, though they must give quarter to those that are unarmed.

As soon as the enterprise succeeds, and the garrison is taken, all the prisoners must be brought together in the market-places, the commander and officers separated from the common men, who must be searched, and even their knives taken from them, and be ordered to sit down, and behave peaceably. Parties are hereupon sent to every street to collect the horses and baggage of the enemy, and by the division of which, the common men must be encouraged to further good behaviour. The two detachments which have had their posts in front of the Heitzer and Holzthor now advance, and the prisoners and booty go off, under a sufficient guard, by the road which leads over Meerholz to Hanau, being the nearest and the most secure.

A signal is given near Altenhasslau to the detachment, which stood behind Rhode towards Budingen, and as soon as this arrives and the prisoners have advanced a league or a league and a half, the town may be abandoned, and you may retire likewise by the road over Meerholz towards Hanau, upon which the fifty cavalry and the reserve, who are near Altenhasslau, and have rested during the attack, bring up the rear. But should an enemy's detachment be hastened to this neighbourhood, every means must be employed to expedite your retreat and to gain Meerholz. Should the enemy in his pursuit overtake you, halt with the rear upon the mountain near Meerholz, where the count's shooting-house stands, and face the enemy. For if you are forced to fight with the enemy, after a successful enterprise, you must rather sacrifice a handful of men, than lose all that you have gained. But in order to hazard nothing by this undertaking, you may previously send on the same day a strong detachment from Hanau, as far as the country of Newhazlau, whereby the retreat will be fully secured.

It may also happen, that a post, which is intended to be surprised, is reinforced, contrary to your expectations. If you are so near it, that you cannot make an honourable retreat, you must not be depressed, but attack with resolution, as this is the only means of concealing your inferior force from the enemy. For example; In the year 1758, during the expedition which Prince Henry undertook against the Hildesheimens and the people of Brunswick, the Prussian Major Bork received the intelligence that 100 French were in the Hanoverian village of Eldagsen.

On the 3rd March, at daybreak, he rushed into the village with 120 hussars and *yägers*; but instead of finding only 100 men there, he met with the whole Hussar regiment of Berchiny, who stood ready saddled and bridled on the other side of the village; nevertheless he made an attack with the greatest bravery, routed the whole regiment with his few men, cut down many and took one captain of a troop and 12 men prisoners.

Sixth Section.
Of the duty of a Partisan on the Retreat of the Enemy.

The enemy's retreat may be either wilful or forced; but neither case can escape the eye of at partisan, who understands his duty, and possesses the necessary alertness. He should place himself as near the enemy as possible, in order to follow him closely as soon as he moves. He must first of all endeavour to take some prisoners, in order to learn where the enemy directs his march. He must annoy the enemy, retard his march, and take advantage of the least disorder that he may perceive. But he must be circumspect how he proceeds, for fear of losing his corps, which, in such occurrences, may very easily happen.

In these cases there are many advantages on his side, since it may be concluded, that every soldier who retreats, is dissatisfied. the common man, who cannot discover the secret intentions of the general, loses a part of his courage as soon as he begins to retreat. On the contrary, those who pursue the enemy are animated by the hope of gaining a large booty, their courage encreases by every step, they look with contempt upon their enemy, who flee before them, and they consider themselves from this moment as superior to him: soldiers at such a time will perform all that bravery is capable of; when pursuing the enemy I never wanted volunteers, though ever so tired, for the thoughts of booty gave them new strength. On the contrary, on a retreat, I have seldom dared to request more duty, even from the bravest, than they were bound to perform.

If the retreat of an enemy be forced, a partisan has already half gained his point. This is a fine opportunity for him, to shew his ability in sight of both armies, especially if he find troops following to support him in case of necessity. In this he may perform brilliant feats, if he know how to employ the moment to the greatest advantage. In such an opportunity, send, in the night time, small parties of *yägers* towards the enemy's camp, who endeavour to draw so near to the sentries on their hands and feet, that they can see the watch fire, and may soon discover when the sentries go off, whereupon as soon as they observe this, they must fire upon the watch-fire, which will serve as a signal, that the enemy are retiring.

This firing, as laughable as it may appear, has however a great influence upon the retiring soldiers, since they conclude from it, how dangerous and toilsome the following day will be. Colonel Morgan followed this method, when the British army was forced to retreat from Philadelphia through the Jerseys. I had the piquet, on the day when the army, on this retreat, had encamped in the country of Altentown, and the custom of the piquet making the advance and rear guards having been introduced in the *yäger* corps by Colonel Wurmb, I was silently recalling the piquets from their posts to form the rear-guard, when the American riflemen, who, during the whole night had been swarming round the camp, fired in the midst of our watch-fire.

At daybreak, when they could see us, they hung upon us and accompanied our march to the new camp. Colonel Wurmb was obliged to support me several times with his corps and the light infantry. The piquets consisted of about 200 men, and notwithstanding we always marched through woody countries, I lost only about 60. The American Colonel Butler once followed this rule with success; it was, when Sir William Howe, in the beginning of the campaign of 1777, retreated from New-Brunswick to Ambay, with an intention to decoy General Washington out of his strong position, near. Moristown. This partisan had placed himself so near to the English army, in the night time, that at the moment the rear-guard was going to follow the army, Wreed's *yäger* company was so violently fallen. upon, that had Captain Wreed lost his presence of mind, the whole would certainly have been destroyed. We had to march five leagues, with but little heavy artillery, and no baggage, and yet we did not arrive. in the camp near Ambay until dark.

The Americans hung so close upon the rear-guard, that the English army were several times forced to face about I was detached under General Leslie to the Scotch Hill, in order to gain this pass, which the army must inevitably have gone through. I found here also the riflemen beforehand, and though the ground gave us much advantage, yet we lost many men on this day, which proves, how necessary it is to have strong corps of good riflemen in an army.

This is the time when riflemen are to be employed, having the advantage, that their rifles carry farther than muskets, and can do more execution on the enemy at a distance, being themselves out of his reach.

The riflemen ought to follow the enemy in small parties of 20 or 30 men at the distance of five or six hundred paces. These parties must again divide, by two's or three's, and endeavour, if the country permit, to come between the enemy's flanks and the columns. Their fire must not be directed upon the flankers, but between them, upon the corps. For, if by its elevated direction, the shot should not effectually kill, yet it will disable many for some time; and the fight of a great number of wounded will depress the enemy as much as a small number of killed, and a good marksman, at the distance of six or seven hundred paces, never ought to miss a division of cavalry or infantry.

In this manner, if the *yägers* be supported by cavalry and infantry, and the country be so intersected with mountains and woods, they must endeavour to make the enemy pay dear at every step; and when they are conducted by officers who take a pleasure in, and study this part of war, the enemy will hardly be able to retire more than a few leagues in a day.

Should the retreat of the enemy be wilful, and he takes every pre-caution to form his rear-guard of infantry with artillery, *yägers*, dra-goons, and hussars, together, in order that one arm may support the other, and each profit by every advantage which the ground may suc-cessively offer; if he never neglect to cover his flanks, occupy, before-hand, those *defilés* which he must pass, and thereby cover his rear, he may then indeed keep off his pursuers; but not, however, without some loss, if those who are pursuing are daring and resolute, and un-derstand their duty, more especially if the country be so intersected, that the retreating party be forced to take the high road.

In the beginning of the year 1777, when Lord Cornwallis quar-tered in and about New-Brunswick, in order to supply the want of meat and forage, he was frequently forced to make inroads into the enemy's quarters; we had always indeed the good fortune to obtain our end, but had hardly retired a few paces, than the Americans were sure to appear, and accompany us so warmly to our quarters, that we paid dear enough each time for our little beef and forage, though, we retreated in the best order.

If you know the country, you may easily gain the start, to alarm the middle of one of the enemy's columns, on his retreat. In the retreat of the English army from Montmouth-Court-house in New-Jersey, which march lay through very strong thickets. General Lee was to take, with an American corps, to the right of the flank of the English army, whilst General Washington was to attack the rear-guard of Gen-eral Clinton, when passing a *defilé*, of which both sides were covered with swampy thickets; but the attack of General Lee being very flow, the well-projected plan of General Washngton was wholly frustrated, and his advance-guard not being supported by the attack of General

Lee, was defeated.

I must; not forget mentioning the retreat of the Prussian army, under the Prince of Prussia, from Bömish Lippa to Zittau, and the march of the king to the siege of Olmütz, through Bohemia, in both of which I am surprised at the inactivity of the Austrians, who, having so great a number of their best light troops in their army, should have suffered the Prussians to march through a country so intersected, and in so short a time, with the small loss that they sustained. Though the measures of that great king, and of his skilful and active generals, might have been ever so excellent, and well obeyed, yet had the Austrian Hussars and Croats been more active, the Prussians would have suffered more than they really did; for the countries through which the Prussians had to pass, were so interfered with woods and *defilés*, that every step should have cost some lives,

It is also astonishing, that Sir William Howe suffered the Americans, after the Battle of Brandywine River, to retreat so easily, and gain the Chulkil. The Anspach and Hessian *yägers*, supported by both battalions of the English light infantry, and both regiments of light dragoons, had been sufficient to ruin in such a manner the American army, who fled in the greatest haste, that it could not have appeared again during the whole campaign. But instead of profiting by this favourable moment, the British Commander contented himself with the honour of having routed the enemy, and rested three days on the field of battle, during which time the Americans gained the Chulkil.

If you perceive any disorder in the retreat of the enemy, that one arm be not properly supported by another, or that a part of the rear be too far distant from the other, or you find that he has neglected to cover his flanks; in any of these cases, fall upon him without delay. Endeavour to gain the heights and thickest woods in such mountainous countries with your *yägers*, who must incessantly accompany the enemy, and keep up a well-aimed fire, which will harass him, cost him many men, and retard his march. I have very often seen, during the American war, a handful of riflemen hinder our march, embarrass us, and have also remarked, how difficult it was to injure these men who individually annoyed our columns, and advance and rear-guards; I have seen few of these men killed, and we, on the contrary, always lost many; and supposing they were even driven back, they however, appeared again in a short time.

If these riflemen had been better disciplined, and conducted by officers as perfectly acquainted with the particular management of this kind of warfare, as they already were with the country and inhabitants, I am firmly of opinion, that the English would have been forced to have given up the war in the second year, and Washington would not have been obliged to have fought a single battle.

But in pursuing the enemy, care must be taken not to fall into one of his snares. For example, after the Battle of Wilhelmsthal, when the allied and French armies were separated by the Fulde, Baron Wintzingeroda remained at New-Morschen, with the Hessian *yägers*, in order to observe the enemy's corps, which was at Old-Morschen. It was supposed that the French would retire in a short time,, for which reason Wintzingeroda was upon his guard, to prevent the enemy from retiring unperceived. The day before the French intended to leave their camp, they let their camp and watch-fires go out in the night, broke up their tents, and concealed themselves behind the heights of Old-Morschen.

Baron Wintzingeroda, who perceived the alterations in the enemy's camp the same night, crossed the Fulda at daybreak, in order to follow the enemy, but he had hardly approached near to the enemy's camp, than he received such a heavy artillery fire, that those of his corps were happy who could regain the right bank of the Fulda. Fortunately for the Hessian *yägers*, the French artillery began to open too soon, for the advance guard of Wintzingeroda was scarcely in the abandoned camp of Turpin's hussars, than they began to fire. If the French had suffered the *yägers* to advance nearer, and had fallen upon them with the cavalry, which was concealed on the flank of their battery, the moment they had fired, the greater part of the *yägers* would certainly never have reached the Fulda.

When Washington found that Sir William Howe intended to retire from Ambay to Staaten Island, he placed Lord Sterling with a corps of light troops nearly in front of the British camp, in order to fall upon the rear-guards before their passage; Lord Sterling, who supposed that the: English, army had already crossed Prince's Bay, and the rear guard only were near Ambay, fell upon the *yäger* corps in the afternoon with great courage, but as his opponent was prepared for the reception, he was forced to retreat, after a considerable loss of killed and prisoners.

If a partisan think that a battle must take place in a short time, he should request pemrission from his commanding general to make an attempt upon the flanks or rear of the enemy. His march must be as secret as possible, and he should place himself in such a manner on the sides of the enemy, that if he be routed, one of the passes which the enemy must take will be in his hands. By such an opportunity a part of the baggage may be seized, and the trouble well paid.

If the retreat of the enemy happen in open countries, pursue him with cavalry, and support these with infantry; for should he fall upon the cavalry, they can retire upon the infantry. It is best, if the ground permit, for the cavalry to march in two lines, having intervals of the same space which each troop occupies. The second line follows at the distance of 300 paces, each troop of this line placed opposite to the intervals of the first line, in order to support it. The flank troops of the second line must however outwing those of the first by their whole front, and in case the enemy should hazard an attack, or you overtake him, these must endeavour to turn his flanks. The troops of the first line have their flankers in front, who follow the enemy, continually firing their pistols or carbines; mounted riflemen may also be employed to annoy and create confusion in the enemy's squadrons, by a well-directed fire.

A few *yägers* may also be mixed with them, to do more execution. Should the enemy's cavalry rout yours, the *yägers* must endeavour to save themselves through the intervals, and should they even find themselves in the midst of the enemy's cavalry, they must throw themselves flat upon the ground, and remain there until the enemy's cavalry retire again, who will not certainly make a long stay, nor run the rifle of so much danger, merely for the sake of cutting down a few *yägers*. The latter spring up the moment they find the enemy retire, and follow him with a well-aimed fire. If *yägers* were trained and accustomed to this method of fighting, few would ever be lost. In general, though the enemy may retreat in the greatest order, yet not a day can pass that he will not lose some men, if those who pursue him be skilful, cool, and collected.

In the American war, I have observed that this manoeuvre was always executed with great indexterity by the English; it appeared, as if they were not acquainted with it, and were always glad to see the enemy retire. The day when Fort Lee was taken by the English, I requested permission from a certain general now living, (as at time of first publication), to hang upon the American column, who were retiring before our eyes, from Fort Lee to Hackensack, and gave us an opportunity of attacking the right flank of their march: but I was refused, though the nature of the ground was such, that 100 *yägers* could have ruined that column. At New Brunswick, when General Washington crossed the Rariton, and at Trainton, when he crossed the

Delaware; at Rhode Island, when General Sulivan made his retreat to New England, and at German Town, we always built a golden bridge for our enemy. This is indeed acting in a Christian-like manner, but it is not doing justice to our king and country, for the principal duty of a general is to put an end to the war as soon as possible.

SECTION 7
OF AMBUSCADES.

Though the rules laid down for surprisals, are similar to those for ambuscades, yet it will be useful to give general rules, in order to direct the conduct of the partisan. They are as follow:

1. Regulate your ambuscade according to the strength of the enemy, and the nature of the ground. If the country be even, employ cavalry, or both arms at the same time; on the contrary, in countries much intersected, light infantry must be employed to the utmost of their ability.

2. Use well disciplined troops, who are not inclined to desertion, and who can be depended upon for the greatest silence.

3. The troops must be conducted into the ambuscade in such a manner, that their footsteps cannot be traced, *viz.* be marched to the spot from the side, opposite to which you intend to fall upon the enemy.

4. Ambuscades must not be laid too soon; men who are forced to remain motionless will suffer doubly, from the excessive heat of the weather, and if it be in a severe winter, their limbs become benumbed: in this state they will be unable to move on the approach of the enemy, and their spirits be depressed proportionably to the stiffness of their joints.

5. Ambuscades must be laid double, treble, and fourfold, in order to fall upon the enemy on different sides, by which he will have no time to collect himself, or retreat in order.

6. A reserve must be kept to send assistance to that place, where the enemy may defend himself most resolutely.

7. The men must be so placed, that they be ready for action. If they lay down upon the ground, it must be done in the same order and disposition as when they stood up.

8. The men must have bread and water with them, and the cavalry must have one feed at least.

9. The officers and non-commissioned officers commanding divisions, must have their attention fixed upon their men, as well upon the march as during the ambuscade, that no soldier may go off; and all the servants, as they are generally inclined to maraud, must be conducted and watched by an officer, and some trusty non-commissioned officers.

10. Horses that neigh, dogs accustomed to bark, or men who cough or have colds, must not be employed in ambuscades.

11. Those soldiers whose fidelity you are fully assured of, must be used for sentries. These may be placed in trees, or they may lay themselves flat on the ground, and by a signal previously agreed upon, announce the approach of the enemy. For example, give the sentries white handkerchiefs, to make the concerted signal, by shewing them from behind their backs, but this must be done very near the ground; the commander of the ambuscade must choose a place for his post from whence he can immediately discover this signal. It is best to send officers or trusty non-commissioned officers as sentinels.

12. All the inhabitants, &c. who pass the ambuscade within a certain distance, and whom you suppose may have discovered it, must be seized.

13. The enemy must not be wholly surrounded, more especially if you are inferior to him in strength, for it might excite him to a desperate resistance.

There are few countries in the world, which do not afford places for ambuscades. In even countries, corn fields, villages, and farms, may be occupied. The most open countries have frequently favoured the success of ambuscades, being the least expected in such places. In intersected countries, there are woods, thickets, valleys, ravines, hollow ways, uneven grounds, and ditches, in and behind which a number of men can be easily concealed.

The principal reasons for laying ambuscades are as follow:

1. To attack, carry off, or destroy an enemy's convoy, the march of which has been ascertained, and which you may not conceive yourself sufficiently strong to attack openly.

2. To draw an enemy's detachment that has often annoyed you into a snare, and to destroy him.

3. To hinder the enemy in foraging.

4. To seize couriers with important dispatches, or otherwise principal persons of the enemy's army.

5. During retreats, to get rid of a close pursuit.

In the first case, three or four different ambuscades must be laid, one of which will serve as a reserve, by which the part that meets the greatest resistance may be supported. Three ambuscades must be so laid, that the head, the centre, and the rear of the enemy can be attacked at the same moment with vigour. In the attack, detach small parties of cavalry to the intervals, in order to amuse those of the enemy who march along the convoy, and who might collect and support those parts of the convoy which might be attacked, observing that your parties of cavalry do not engage in serious action, but only skirmish with the enemy. Those however who are in the real attack, must not lose their time by firing, but after the first volley charge the enemy with fixed bayonets, at the same time giving a loud shout, in order to spread confusion throughout the whole.

If you have certain intelligence, when and where the enemy intend to forage, lay in that country different ambuscades of cavalry, supported by infantry, who, should the enemy neglect the necessary precaution, must rush at once upon the escort of the foragers, drive them back, and endeavour to penetrate even amidst the foragers. You must endeavour to kill as many men and horses as possible, take with you what you can, and retreat as quick as you advanced. As with troops not well disciplined, the servants, as well as the soldiers of the escort, endeavour by this opportunity to go marauding, it will be very easy to take a number of men and horses: such marauders, who often commit the most shocking barbarities in the villages, at which humanity shudders, must be cut down, or at least severely beaten, reproaching them with their crimes, in the presence of the inhabitants, by which you recommend yourself, whether it be in an enemy's country or otherwise, and gain the attachment of the whole country.

I cannot conceive, why the Duke of Lauzun, who stood with his legion five leagues from Gloucester, before the allied army undertook the siege of York, suffered the corps near Gloucester to forage quietly, even until the last day. I hardly know any country more adapted for ambuscades, than that from Saul's Plantation to Gloucester Courthouse. All the plantations, which were foraged in this country, are surrounded with thickets, having much underwood, and intelligence of our foraging could not be unknown to the enemy, as every inhabitant of the country was disaffected towards us, and it was always known in camp the evening before, whether the following day should be for foraging.

If you have a knowledge of the character of your enemy's commander, that he be passionate, and yet but a novice in warfare; it may be concluded, that he will be eager to distinguish himself. In this case, it will seldom fail, if you lay an ambuscade, during the night-time, in the neighbourhood of the enemy's outposts, and send at daybreak a small party to annoy them, and the *patroles*, which as soon as attacked, must retreat by the ambuscade; at which time the concealed men must then rush out and cut off the pursuers. But you must, in such case, avoid committing the fault, which a certain lieutenant-colonel did near Gloucester.

It was in the last foraging that was undertaken before the siege of York, I had the advance guard, with 100 cavalry, and as many *yägers* and rangers; I was to set out two hours before daylight, and as soon as I had left Saul's Plantation behind, to extend a chain in order to cover the foraging, during which, in case of an enemy's attack the above mentioned lieutenant-colonel was to support me with 200 cavalry; for Lord Cornwallis had received certain intelligence that the allied army would advance to the siege on the following day; I had scarcely taken the necessary measures, than a small number of French hussars and mounted Virginian volunteers appeared, with whom I skirmished.

The foraging ended fortunately, and Colonel Dundas, who commanded the whole, ordered me to retire, adding, that he had left this lieutenant-colonel with 200 cavalry upon the left of the road as an ambuscade in a thicket, in order to surprise, from thence, the enemy's party, that would certainly pursue me, leaving to me the task of decoying them. I collected my posts, and made the rear with thirty cavalry. The enemy pursued me; I passed by the ambuscade, and the enemy continued hanging upon me; but instead of the commander of the ambuscade having patience a few minutes longer, he sallied out, when only some of the enemy's flankers had passed, by which the plan turned out so unfavourable, that only two volunteers were taken prisoners.

As good and brave soldiers as the British are, yet they are not calculated for the *petite guerre*, for they have not the patience, which is so highly necessary to this tedious and toilsome part of war. In the same campaign, another fault of this kind frustrated a plan in which I had nearly succeeded. It was in the country of Greatbridge, where

General Arnold had entrenched a post which covered the pass from Portsmouth towards North Carolina; the general had received intelligence, that the enemy intended to carry this post: To prevent which, a detachment of 500 men was sent there in order to strengthen it. The detachment had hardly arrived, when information was received, that the enemy was on his march with 1500 men, had artillery, and were provided with fascines and ladders. Having been some time before in this country with Colonel Simcoe, beyond Camp's Landing, I remarked, that only one road led out of North Carolina on that side to this post, which had been made about a small league distant by help of a dyke, through an impenetrable morass, and which ran zigzag for 800 or 1000 paces; this road onwards from the dyke, as far as within a quarter of a league from Greatbridge, was bordered on both sides with thickets; in consequence, I requested permission from the commander of the detachment, to lay myself in ambuscade in the thicket which was along the road before daybreak.

I obtained leave, and took a reinforcement of as many British, as made up 250 men with my *yägers*; I arrived two hours before day-light near the dyke, divided my detachment in four equal parts, laid two ambuscades on each side of the road, that on the left nearly upon the dyke, and that upon the right 100 paces farther up, in order that the firing of the one division might not injure the other. 400 or 500 paces farther from the dyke I laid in the same manner, two other ambuscades, and placed the greater part of my riflemen in the ambuscade nearest the dyke, in order to create more confusion among the enemy by a destructive fire; I stationed a double post; of infantry at the distance of a musket-shot from the dyke, where I remained myself to command the first firing, which was to be as a signal for the ambuscades to fall upon the enemy after the first volley, and at the same time to give a loud shout; for my intention was, to suffer 500 or 600 men to pass the dyke, all of whom would certainly have been lost; for those who were behind them, on account of the length and narrowness of the dyke, could have afforded no assistance, and would certainly have taken flight to avoid the snare into which their comrades had fallen.

I had given orders for all small *patroles* of the enemy to pass unmolested. About ten o'clock in the forenoon, a *patrole* of four riflemen appeared, who perceiving the sentries, returned over the dyke.

The enemy not appearing in the afternoon, the commander of the detachment was impatient, and called me off. I requested permission to remain until evening, but he ordered me a second time to leave the place, that the whole was a false alarm, and that he intended to *patrole* towards the enemy. I had hardly drawn up my ambuscade, and my commander just arrived with the remaining part of the detachment, than a detachment of the enemy appeared, but which, after perceiving the red coats, retreated precipitately over the dyke; a part of the cavalry pursued, and took an officer of the dragoons, whose horse had fallen down with him. I experienced only disappointment as a recompense for my trouble, and we marched back again the same evening.

If you be often annoyed, especially in winter quarterly, it is easy, by well laid ambuscades, to tire out the enemy. This must not however be done immediately upon his having alarmed you once or twice, but let him become daring, which will certainly be the case, if you permit different parties to go here and there unmolested. For example: during the winter in the beginning of 1777, when the corps under Lord Cornwallis were quartered in and round New Brunswick, the cordon, more especially that of the *yäger* posts, was daily alarmed by the Americans, who, elated by the affair of Trainton, had become very daring.

The cordon of these quarters formed a circle, of which Brunswick was the centre, and the River Rariton the diameter, which (in the vicinity of my post at Landing), was not more than 100 paces wide. The left wing of my post extended to the left bank of this river, where it had a ford which I kept occupied in the daytime by a double post, but from which I retired in the night, as it lay too far out of my chain towards the enemy. On the opposite side of the river to this post was a parsonage-house, having a barn behind it, by which the high road led from Rocky Hill to Brunswick. The Americans had discovered by spies, that before I occupied this post in the morning, I searched this country as far as the river, where there were different ravines, in which the enemy might have concealed himself in the night-time: a number of riflemen, as the spring was then approaching, had several nights sneaked along one after the other into the above-mentioned barn, from whence they fired, as soon as the *patroles* approached the river, by which one *yäger* was severely wounded.

As I was not inclined (out of humanity to the priest, though he was no loyalist), to burn down the barn; and as I wished to get rid of these visitors, who would probably have killed many more brave *yägers*, (who made up the strength of both, the first companies, which Captain Wreden and I had brought to America, and who were already reduced from 250 to about 120), I had recourse to an ambuscade, which fully answered our purpose. Each company was provided with a light two-pounder.

The night before I laid the ambuscade, I took the cannoneer, shewed him the place where the field piece should be conducted, I made him three signals by white rods, of three different shots which he was to fire one after the other, as soon as he should hear a shot from the barn. On the road where the field piece was to be placed, was a thin hedge, which I ordered to be made so thick in the night-time, that the field piece could not be seen through it. Before daybreak, I ordered it to be drawn to the intended place, under an escort, and I placed Lieutenant Trautetter (who, in bravery had scarcely his equal, and who was a great loss to the corps, being afterwards killed at Brandy Wine River), with 30 *yägers*, on the bank of the river beyond the barn, with directions to keep his eye upon the door of it; and as the left bank of the river was here bordered with meadows, the *yägers* were to lie flat upon the ground, and not shew themselves before the Americans should be dislodged from the barn by the artillery.

At daybreak I made a *patrole*, and as soon as I approached the river, a few shots were fired from the barn. The artilleryman began to fire, and on the third shot the enemy's detachment rushed out. As soon as the *yägers* in the ambuscade perceived it, they rose up, and directed their fire so well, that the greater part of the enemy's party was either killed or wounded; and from that time we remained unmolested.

One may also decoy an enemy into an ambuscade, by driving herds of cattle or a number of waggons, in the neighbourhood of the enemy's post, and laying an ambuscade at some distance, which rushes out immediately, when the enemy believes himself master of the booty. The farther you are from the enemy, the more easily such plan will succeed; but those who drive the cattle, or conduct the waggons, must be resolute soldiers, dressed like country people; for servants or peasantry would not hazard themselves so neat the enemy, or would perhaps run away too soon.

Much as ambuscades frighten the enemy, and give the soldiers a relish for the *petite guerre* when successful, yet the more care must be taken that they be not laid too often, and fall out contrary to your wish, in which case the confidence of the soldiers will be easily alienated from their commander. The principal rule is, to know your enemy and the country. But should an ambuscade be laid in vain, retire from it with the greatest silence without being discovered by any one, and not follow the example of that man, whom Colonel Wurmb placed in ambuscade in the campaign of 1779, in the churchyard near Philips Bridge, and ordered, if the enemy did not appear, to return silently at daybreak. The enemy did not appear, and the dextrous partisan called back his sentries with the bugle. It appears scarcely probable, but I heard it with my own ears.

SECTION 8

OF RETREATS.

Every retrograde march, whether wilful or forced, is a retreat. The first is not subject to so great difficulties, since you have time to consider before-hand what measures to take afterwards; but in the latter, it is quite otherwise ; the enemy in general gives you no time, he hangs upon you before you can collect yourself; he is generally superior in force; his soldiers, who have gained some advantage, believe themselves better and stronger, and are more daring, than yours, who by being continually annoyed, become weary and dissatisfied.

I will now consider retreats which are made before a pursuing enemy of a superior force. Here the commander of a corps or detachment may shew his talents, his skill and knowledge in the art of war, and his courage. The hero shews himself in his real greatness; and ancient as well as modern history, never bestow greater eulogiums upon generals, than in their descriptions of brilliant retreats.

The success of a retreat depends entirely upon a knowledge of the country, understanding how to employ and place your troops, that one may defend and support the other; and in knowing how to take an immediate resolution in every occurrence and alteration, in order to resist the impetuosity of the enemy.

The situation of the country may render one retreat more toilsome than another: in an open country the motions of the enemy may be seen at a distance, and his intentions often frustrated. But in a mountainous country, or one intersected with woods, it is far more difficult, since every stratagem and manoeuvre may be employed; and I again repeat, that it is absolutely necessary to endeavour to acquire the most perfect knowledge of the country in which war is carried on, so that at every step backwards, you may always know before-hand where cavalry, infantry, or artillery, should be employed separately, and where they can be used together.

The course of rivers should be known; you must be acquainted with the bridges, fords, and *defilés* in your rear. You ought to consider before-hand where ambuscades can be laid, by which you can retard the enemy, but ought to be certain of your advantage before you undertake them, so as not to engage without necessity. You must know more than one road, and make use of your ingenuity to alter, or form plans, according to circumstances.

If the retreat happen in an open country, your welfare depends upon the accuracy of your dispositions. In this case, place your corps in a line, the light infantry in the centre, leaving intervals between each company for platoons of riflemen, and place the cavalry in eight divisions, on both flanks of the infantry. As soon as the signal for the retreat be given, all even divisions must retire to a certain distance, and halt and front; the odd divisions who during this opposed the enemy, and covered their retreat, having their skirmishers two or three hundred paces in front, and on both flanks, and the riflemen must now be in extended order; this line retires, as soon as the other has formed, under cover of the fire of their flankers, marches through the intervals of the standing line, and forms up in the same manner as the first at a certain distance.

In this manner one line retreats through the other, until the enemy has given up the pursuit But the flankers of the cavalry and riflemen of that part which stands formed up, must, when the advancing line is only one hundred paces from it, fall out, to support and relieve those who are skirmishing. The retreating line calling in again their flankers and riflemen, when they have passed one hundred paces through the intervals of those that are, formed up. If the flankers be pressed too hard by the enemy, they must retreat towards the divisions that have remained formed, and the standing line moves up in order to gain the intervals.

In this case the riflemen must lose no time, but form up in the intervals purposely left for them. The two troops on the wings retire to the distance of one or two hundred paces, in order to cover both flanks, and to fall upon those of the enemy's cavalry on his attack; these troops must not, however, place themselves behind the line, but so as to outwing the line, by their whole front. In this posture you may, if you are forced to fight, wait the enemy's approach; but it is better to go and meet him, if he be not far distant; for a resolute movement forward gives courage to your soldiers and embarrasses the enemy, by its being unexpected.

Should some parties of the enemy pursue so far from their main body, that they cannot be immediately supported, you must take advantage of this favourable moment, and fall upon them. But, as soon as you have chastised their imprudence, make your retreat in the former order.

If you find on your march, bushies, ponds, or ravines, or be proceeding near the banks of rivers, draw towards them for *appui*, and make your disposition accordingly. For instance, close your infantry to a pond, ravine, or river, covering the other flank with cavalry, but a bush or a small thicket must be occupied by your infantry, or only your riflemen, and the cavalry should be placed near. Upon the whole, take every advantage of the ground.

Should you be pursued by a superior number of cavalry, the infantry must retire by column of subdivisions, and your cavalry be placed in two lines *en echequier* on both wings, covered by the fire of the infantry who can form up and front, on all sides, by this disposition. Supposing the corps or detachment, which is forced to retreat, before a superior number of cavalry, to consist of 2000 infantry and 1000 cavalry, I would divide the infantry into two columns, and my cavalry into two divisions, one of which should be placed between the head, and the other between the rear of both columns.

In this disposition there will be no difficulty in moving; you can front on all sides with rapidity, the cavalry is covered by the fire of the infantry, they can act with security when a favourable opportunity offers, and can find support every moment; the infantry in such situation, will be attacked by cavalry with difficulty; I think that this disposition would be the most favourable, if you should be forced to retreat before a swarm of Tartars or Cossacks. Should you have artillery in such a case, it must be drawn on the flanks of the head and rear of both columns.

If you find that you cannot withstand a superior force of cavalry, order yours to save themselves by flight, and having formed the square, retreat with your infantry; for it is better to lose a part than the whole, a party of infantry being sooner replaced than good cavalry. For example, after the winter expedition in 1760, when the allied army left the Wetterau, gave up the sieges of Cassel and Ziegenheyn, and returned into Westphalia, General Luckner, with his hussar regiment and the Schlotheim grenadier battalion, which consisted of 4 grenadier companies of the Hessian guards, was fallen upon on his retreat by more than 30 squadrons of French cavalry.

This celebrated, skilful and great partisan immediately perceived, that at last it must be his fate to be either taken prisoner or cut to pieces. He therefore resolved to save himself and his hussars. Colonel Schlotheim, who could not follow with his grenadiers, formed the square, and retreated in the best order from Kalbsburg, over the Plain, to Fritzlar, without loss. As he was one of those rare men, who do not sound their own heroic deeds in every ear, but who content themselves with a consciousness of their own worth, a certain person, known at headquarters by his *bonmots*, attributed the whole merit of this admirable retreat to himself. He received the compliment for it, and, if I am not mistaken, a present; but to his shame, the truth was discovered. I think that such a man deserves the punishment due to a common thief; for what robber can be more infamous than he, who steals that honour and reputation which another has dearly purchased at the *risqué* of his liberty and his life.

As I have advised infantry to form the square in retreating before a superior force of cavalry, and have given this example of Colonel Schlotheim, it may be objected that this is no proof of that effect of such disposition of infantry against cavalry, the French cavalry not having crossed their sabers with the bayonets of these grenadiers, and that perhaps any other cavalry could have crushed this battalion. Though I have served in the infantry from my youth, I must grant, that if the Duke of Broglio, who was present himself, had hazarded a squadron, these brave grenadiers would in the end have been sacrificed; and I think moreover, that the best infantry, though the square may preserve ever so good an order, cannot stand the charge of good cavalry; for a skilful commander of cavalry will regulate his attack at a distance, in such a manner that they will only be exposed to the fire of one side of the square.

This attack must be made by the cavalry in column, and if the first troop be destroyed by the fire or the bayonets, yet the following will cut down all before them, and the horses themselves, when they have the bayonets in their breasts, cannot be kept off by the infantry, for being so animated, they do not feel the pain of their wounds. I have experienced a proof of this myself. In the affair of Crutches Mill, in the campaign of 1777, my horse was wounded in the body, but my servant did not perceive it, until the evening after the action; and though it had received the shot early in the morning, it nevertheless carried me through the whole day.

I will now cite two examples in favour of cavalry: First. In the campaign of 1759, as the Austrians, under General de Ville, wished to drive off General Fouquet from his strong post near Landshut in Silesia, the latter sent Major Franclin to occupy the small town of Freyburg with

200 men, in order to maintain the communication with Schweidnitz. On the approach of the Austrians, the major was forced to leave this post, having no orders to defend himself against a superior force at the risque of his last man. He endeavoured to retreat to Schweidnitz, and intended at first to march along the Pölsnitz, but as he was overtaken and surrounded on this march by the Austrian cavalry, he determined, with great presence of mind, to attempt the last resource, and formed the square.

He expected to pass the plain, and attain a thicket, called the Nonnenbush, but before he could reach it, he was several times attacked by the Austrian cavalry, whom however he repulsed and drove back each time, by a well-directed fire. The Austrian general, who was not far distant, hearing the fire of the small arms, hastened with more cavalry, and renewed the attack, whereby, in the end, this handful of brave Prussians, having fired away all their ammunition, and being wholly exhausted, was forced to yield. The Austrian general, who esteemed merit even in an enemy, stopped the fury of the cavalry, saved the lives of many of these brave men, and honoured the Prussian major, and all under his command, with the highest praise.

Secondly. In the same war, a Saxon battalion retreated, not far from Langensalza, in the best order, before the Hessian dragoon guards, under the then Colonel Heister. They directed their fire so well at every attack, that the dragoons were repulsed each time with great loss; But as the colonel, fully assured of the bravery of his dragoons, would not relinquish his design, he renewed the attack, and the whole Saxon battalion was in a few minutes cut to pieces.

As these two examples are illustrative of the advantage of cavalry, I must now mention one, which will prove the possibility of infantry, in the before-mentioned disposition, being able to withstand the best cavalry. It was when the Swedes, in the year 1758, entered the Prussian dominions, and General Wedel, after the Russians had been routed, near Zorndorf, by the King of Prussia, hastened there with his corps, in order to drive out the Swedes from Brandenburgian and Prussian Pomerania. The Prussian general received intelligence on his march, that a Swedish detachment had advanced over Fehrbellin, in order to forage.

The general, on this information, took Moring's hussars, and Pletting's dragoons, and found the reserve of the Swedes near Terrau, which consisted of 100 cavalry and 200 infantry; the Swedish cavalry attacked the advance guard of the Prussians with the greatest courage, but were routed; the Swedish infantry, finding themselves without the support of their cavalry, formed the square, and retreated towards Fehrbellein; the Prussian cavalry attacked the square, and charged it several times, but the Swedes, by a well-directed fire, drove them back each time, and many brave hussars and dragoons fell by the point of Swedish bayonets. This example is particularly instructive upon the question, and has scarcely its equal in the history of any war.

There being no other resource for the infantry than to form a solid or hollow square, in order to resist cavalry, you must not under such circumstances be depressed, but endeavour by every possible means to save your honour. In this critical moment, encourage your men with a few words, remind them of the brave deeds of their countrymen, and then take your chance; for I have more than once remarked, that fortune favours temerity. If fortune forsake you, it is better to die with honour, than give yourself up as a prisoner with a whole battalion without resistance.

For instance, in the Battle of Hohenfriedberg in 1745, a Saxon grenadier battalion under Lieut. Colonel Schonberg, was separated from the left wing, which it should have covered, by a small thicket, on which its right wing was appuied; the left wing was placed in a thick wood, and upon each wing was a field piece for their protection; 600 paces before the front was a small valley, through which a division could not pass without breaking. In this battle General Froideville of Nassau, which had been only raised three years; as soon as this regiment discovered that the Saxon battalion was separated from the army, they determined to take them prisoners, or cut them to pieces; they therefore quitted the line, passed the valley, and formed again; the Saxons, who were retiring, perceiving the cavalry all at once, resumed their positions, and summoned them to surrender, which the Saxons refused, defying the Prussians with a loud shout; upon which the dragoons began a spirited attack, and though the greater part of the horses were wounded by bayonets, the Saxons were nevertheless cut to pieces in a few minutes.

If the infantry be formed of light infantry and riflemen together, in the manner I have before mentioned, in the plan of a light corps, give your riflemen the second rank in forming the square, who must always endeavour during the march to keep up a well-directed fire upon the approaching cavalry: if the cavalry charge, they must give the first volley at 100 paces distant, which will cost men and horses; the first rank must not fire until it be able to make the enemy feel wadding, ball, and bayonet at once: but it may be possible, that after the riflemen have coolly fired, the courage of the enemy will be abated: perhaps it may be also possible, that the cavalry are shy at the fire of the riflemen, and will give up so dear an attack. I have often been sent in the American war with only *yägers* against the enemy, but was always assured, that if the cavalry braved the fire, it would seldom happen, that their attack was repulsed by the bayonets; I therefore always marched on with confidence, and should have been still more confident with a square of *yägers* against cavalry, than with one of infantry armed with bayonets, which in the present day the soldier carries more for a load and ornament than for defence, and which, from the straightness of the stocks, are very unhandy for firing and charging.

In mountainous countries, the cavalry ought to march before, and the light infantry bring up the rear. The riflemen should endeavour to gain those heights which cover the roads; they must be divided in small parties, and search the mountains on both sides of the road, along which the whole intend to march; they must endeavour to keep off the enemy from the flank, should any of his *patroles* have approached unexpectedly by a narrow path.

If you be overtaken by the enemy in such a circumscribed country, and forced to make a stand, both parties are equal, and the most resolute attack will decide the day, as the enemy, though superior, cannot attack you with a larger front than your own. In this case, if the *defilé* fire can be employed, the light infantry will be able, under its protection, to attack the enemy or retire.

If you perceive that the fire does great execution, charge the enemy with the bayonet; but the moment you have driven him back, endeavour to renew your march in the best order.

If during your retreat in such countries you be continually molested by the enemy, and you know that the country is more open a little farther, send a part of your troops into that country immediately, who must search out a place for an ambuscade there, into which you can decoy the enemy, if pursuing too eagerly. For instance, as the Prussian army under Prince Henry in the campaign of 1758, retreated towards Dresden, and the detached corps at Gamich and Maxen were forced to abandon their posts, the Prussians were continually molested and attacked on their march, in the country of Kesseldorf, by the Croats and hussars of the Austrians.

In order to decoy them into the open field, and get rid of them, the then Lieutenant Colonel Belling placed himself with his hussars in ambuscade in a village that stood on the road side, whilst in the meantime the Croats, who thought their rear secure, advanced nearer and nearer to the plain. The free battalion of Wunsch and a squadron of Meinicke dragoons endeavoured to attack them in front, whereupon the Croats retreated towards the village, in order to secure their rear. Lieutenant Colonel Belling hereupon fell upon them out of his ambuscade, killed or wounded more than 2000, and the Prussians renewed their march afterwards unmolested.

Should you have a river on your rear, and you are forced to pass it by means of a bridge or a ford, make yourself master of it in time, because the enemy will certainly endeavour to gain it, if he understand his duty. In this case, send a party of your cavalry there, who should alight, in order to occupy the opposite bank on both sides of the bridge or ford. If the pass be a *defilé*, occupy the heights at the entrance and issue, in which the mounted riflemen should be employed. Colonel Donop, who was at Montholly during the unfortunate affair at Trenton, sent, the moment he had intelligence of it, Captain Lorey with his few mounted *yägers*, in order to occupy the pass of Croswick, by which General Washington could have cut off the Donop corps from that under Lord Cornwallis, a part of which stood at Princetown.

An officer who is entrusted with such a post, must, as soon as he arrives there, *patrole* the country on the opposite side of the river or *defilé*, to be certain that no enemy is in the neighbourhood, or in case he find the enemy, that he may have time to take proper measures for the defence of his post, which ought to be maintained to the last man. In such an instance, you must not entrust an officer merely by the roster, but appoint one, whose skill, courage, and resolution you are assured of, which will also be the best means to establish emulation among the officers.

The roster according to seniority in a light corps in war time, where the unskilfulness or irresolution of an officer has so frequently occasioned the loss of the honour, liberty, and lives of so many men, has always appeared to me like the electing of a *burgomaster* in a free imperial city, where the municipality assembled round a table, and laid down their honourable heads and grey beards upon it; on the middle of the table was placed a louse, which louse on marching into the beard of one of them, decided the election of the dignity of burgomaster.

If you have a little the advance of the enemy, and you have passed a bridge, ford, or *defilé* in your retreat, you must, should there be a village in the neighbourhood, take some harrows, and throw them into the ford, and stop up the bridge or *defilé* with trees or waggons, two wheels of the latter of which must be taken off. If time permit, and it be a wooden bridge, burn or destroy it. Should the enemy be too near to allow this, kill two or three horses or cows upon the bridge, or in the middle of the *defilé*, by which means you may retard the enemy's cavalry for a short time, since a horse will seldom pass by a dead animal, and the least obstacle gives you an opportunity to continue your advance.

If the enemy hang upon you, and you be forced to retreat in his fight, through such narrow pass, the cavalry must *defilé* first, half of whom must, as soon as they have passed it, dismount, and occupy the bank on both sides of the bridge, or the heights of the *defilé*, in order to cover the passage of the remainder by their fire; the riflemen should follow and support the fire of the cavalry. The light infantry, who form up on this side of the bridge, should fire by files or platoons, to retard the enemy, and must successively retire by files from both flanks, but the centre division in front of the bridge or *defilé* should face about, and fire by files in retreating. The cavalry mount again, the moment the riflemen have spread out on both sides of the pass, and retire from the firing.

If you cannot go round the pass, preserve this disposition until night begins, for the enemy will find it difficult to attack such a pass by force, the gaining of which would cost many men. But should they attempt to take it by force, you must sacrifice some in order to save the greater part In this manner, in the campaign of 1760, General Luckner was forced to sacrifice the grenadier company of the Trumbach thorps, in order to save his hussars and *yägers*; for he had the whole advance guard of the French army upon him at once in a *defilé* near Wildungen. The captain of this company, whose brave grenadiers were either killed or wounded, also saved by his courage and resolution the whole Luckner corps. I am particularly sorry, that I cannot remember the name of this brave man, for no heroic deed should remain hidden from posterity, as nothing excites men more to great actions, than the examples of those distinguished characters, which history records.

How much is it to be wished, that a collection of great military actions were selected from history, to serve as introductory instruction to youth in military colleges: such might be made use of for translations into foreign language, and would certainly be no little stimulus to acts of heroism and magnanimity.

If you form the rear of an army or strong corps, which is forced to retreat, or you cover with your corps either of the flanks, you must employ all your force, in order to be serviceable to the array during the retreat, for as you may always be easily supported, you may hazard more than when you are left alone with a small corps, and have to think of your own safety. In every retrograde step that you take, and in every pass which you are forced to leave, lay all possible obstacles in the way of the enemy, to retard his motions.

If the enemy be delayed in his march by bad and narrow roads, place yourself upon one of the enemy's flanks. For instance. General Maxwell placed himself in the Iron Mountains, near Crutches Mill, in Pennsylvania, and having turned the right flank of Sir William Howe's march, this general was forced to attack and repulse him, before he could proceed any farther, whereby General Washington gained a whole march from the British.

If your army be so closely pressed by the enemy, that a part of the artillery and baggage may be lost, or be so entangled among *defilés*, that it cannot easily proceed, you must rather sacrifice all than flee. In such a case, you must encourage your men, and represent to them that their good conduct will be observed by the whole army, and that this is the moment to gain immortal reputation. It is scarcely credible, what an effect a few energetic words will have upon the soldier, and animate him in these critical circumstances, particularly if the commander appear cheerful and confident: recollect always the old saying, *he who never runs, can never be pursued*. For instance, in a foraging that was undertaken from New Brunswick to Quibeltown, I made the rear after it was ended, with my *yäger* company and a detachment of the English light infantry.

The country was intersected with mountains and thickets; I therefore placed the light infantry in the centre, and the *yägers* upon both flanks: I had scarcely retreated a step than the enemy appeared, and pressed me on all sides. General Leslie rode up to me at the moment when a party of riflemen fell upon my right flank; the general himself thought, that if I were not supported, many men and waggons must be lost. I reached a small height at this moment, which lay in a thick wood: my plan was formed instantly, I ordered the bugle horn to sound the attack, and rushed vigorously upon these *desperadoes*, many fell by the bayonets of the light infantry, and the enemy renounced the pursuit. Lord Cornwallis testified his approbation in general orders, and each *yäger* received a present of a dollar.

Should a corps or detachment, notwithstanding the best disposition, be routed, and its retreat become a flight, my advice is, never to take the common method of rallying, and endeavour to collect the hindmost men for resistance. There is no other resource in this case, than that the commander endeavour to reach the first fugitives, and here begin to form his men, which will be easily done, as they see behind them many more for protection, and if you have only once formed some files, there will be no difficulty in persuading all the following to fall in. But if you will pursue the common method, and cry out *Halt! Stand!* you will only collect a few files, who at last, seeing the others run away, will do the same on the approach of the enemy.

On concluding this small work, I will once more remark, that a commander at the levy or formation of a light corps, and also when war allows him leisure, should endeavour to discipline his men, according to the before described occurrences in war; if he do this, there will be nothing new to his officers and men, he may perform with them whatever is great and noble, and even surmount apparent impossibilities.

Twenty-Three Years Practice and Observations with Rifle Guns

Ezekiel Baker

Contents

RIFLEMAN PRESENTING

Published by E.Baker Gun maker N° 11 White Chapel Road opposite the Church first corner Little Ale Street

Baker's Practice, &c.

One load of powder at all distances should be attended to; no noise or conversation to take place, whilst anyone is presenting or taking aim, as it will take off the attention. The rifle should be held firm in hand, in all positions in presenting to fire: lying on the belly, it will be found difficult for the left hand to grasp the stock forwards; in that case, the sling or belt should be pulled firmly back, to keep the rifle steady while firing, as appears in figures presenting, No. 2 and 3. To fire off hand without a rest; the right foot should be behind the left about 16 inches, the left knee upright and not bent, the right elbow down towards the body, the butt of the rifle in the hollow of the shoulder, the body easily bent forwards, so that the right eye comes over the great toe of the left foot, as figure presenting No. 1.

If the body is more bent, the man will not stand so easy, nor yet so steady; the left hand, when presenting, to be forwards on the swell of the stock, the sling under the elbow, which will make it firm and steady: in presenting to fire and taking aim, both eyes open is best, as by that he will quarter his piece; that will show him when his head is too far over the centre of the stock. The cheek should be pressed on the stock very hard at all times, or the man will deceive himself; for his eye should be as a fixture on the stock every time he takes aim. In taking aim, lay the muzzle of the rifle to the lowest part of the object he means to strike, then bring it up gradually to the part he means to take his aim at: in bringing up the rifle, the fore-finger to be kept light on the trigger, when up to the point intended, he draws the front sight into the notch of the back sight with his eye, as line drawn, figure No. 4. He holds his breath, and pulls gradually without any snatching, as that will alter the direction of the rifle.

In taking aim, sometimes he may hold his breath so long, as will cause a trembling; in that case, the rifle should be taken down, take breath, and aim again: as I never could fire so true, as when I took the first sight. It is a more certain way, to bring the muzzle of the rifle up than down, where the object can be obtained, in bringing the rifle up to the point intended; the cheek is as a fixture on the stock, that when brought to the point, it wants no alteration; but when the muzzle is brought down, it will require the face to be pressed on the stock; in that case the point will be lost, and the man much deceived.

After the trigger is pulled, keep the rifle firm to the shoulder, till the ball strikes the target at 100 yards, this will be known by hearing the ball strike or hit; as that will prevent any startling or throwing back the head, as is often the case in firing. A rifleman should practice to pull the trigger, with a wood driver in the cock, till he can fire off his piece, without starling or shaking the muzzle of his rifle; this is a part that every rifleman should be well acquainted with, as it will make him hare more command of his rifle.

A rifleman to judge of his distance, should be in the habit of stepping his ground, from 1 to 300 paces, or any other distance that may be thought proper; and let him fire at any object at the distance he steps to; by this continual practice, he will learn to measure the distance with his eye to a tolerable certainty at any time; this he should practice in different places, and in all sorts of weather: in windy weather it is necessary a rifleman should practice; which will instruct him what allowance to make from the object to be fired at, either to right or left; as the wind has great power on the ball at long ranges. I have found 300 yards the greatest range I could fire to any certainty. At 300 yards I have fired very well at times, when the wind has been calm. At 400 and 500 yards I have frequently fired, and I have sometimes struck the object; I have aimed as near as possible at the same point; I have found it vary from the point intended: whereas at 200 yards I could have made sure of the point or thereabouts.

For this reason, I am convinced the wind has great power on the ball, after it has passed to a certain distance. I have found it very uncertain to fire over water; if I took the same elevation as on land, the ball dropped short of the object. After trying many experiments of this kind, I never could fire so true as on land. Firing over bogs and swamps I have found to have a similar effect, as firing over water. A rifleman should never use himself to more than one rifle, until he is a compleat master of it; then he may use any one for the information of others. In loading with a ball, be careful that the ball is in the middle of the patch of leather, or greased rag provided for that purpose, before it is rammed down the barrel; if it is more on one side than the other, it will have an inclination to throw the ball from the straight line; both sides of the patch greased is the best, in hurry of loading, there can be no mistake.

A ball forced down too hard or yet too easy, I never found to go so true, as when properly fitted; the ball with its patch should fit air tight, or it will not have the desired effect. Be careful the ball is rammed home to the powder, and with as little bruising as possible; every rifleman should mark his rammer at the muzzle end of barrel when loaded, which will shew him when the ball is close down on the powder. At all times care should be taken, that the hammer is shut down upon the pan, before the ball is rammed down, or the air the ball drives before it, will blow all the powder out of the touch-hole. If by mistake that should happen, the ball must be drawn out with a screw turned into the end of the rammer, and provided for that purpose: under the head of the rammer is a small hole made to put in a lever, which makes the rammer similar to a carpenters' gimblet, and forms a purchase to screw into the ball, and by that means draws the ball out of the barrel.

After firing a few rounds, it will be found difficult to draw the ball out; to remedy this, I have found the following method to have the desired effect. Pour a little water down the barrel, which will loosen the filth, and the ball will be drawn with ease; it may happen that water at such time cannot be got, if the man can make urine and apply it in the same way, it will have the same effect; after the ball is drawn, it will stick fast on the screw as the fingers cannot unscrew it, then lay the ball on a stone or hard ground, and strike it with the butt end of the rifle to flatten it, which will be taken off with ease; the barrel should be wiped dry before loaded again.

Rifles throwing to the right or left, is sometimes owing to the trigger pulling too hard, and at other times, to the man throwing his head too far over the centre of the stock, which causes a cross-sight. The trigger should not be pulled so hard as to alter the direction of the rifle in firing. If the rifle is found to throw to the right, the back sight should be drove to the left, and the front sight to the right; the sights are left loose for that purpose. If it throws to the left, move the sight contrary as above, till the man who uses it finds it right. I have no opinion of the folding elevating sights; the sight for the greatest range may be up, when a shot at a shorter distance may offer; in that case, the man not perceiving it, would be much deceived at his intended object;

besides it will require the face taken from its stationary place on the stock, for the eye to pass over it: in that a man will be deceived, as he will have no rest for his cheek.

In trying off guns, I have been deceived by the folding elevating sights, for which reason I have found one sight most certain to be depended upon at all distances; and that its shape, on the top a sphere of a circle, with a small notch in the centre, so as to admit of the light on each side of the front sight, which forms itself to the eye, better than any eight I have ever yet tried; the back sight should not stand so near the lock, as it will be liable to be filled with smoak from the pan, which will be a great denial to taking a true sight through the small notch. For if a man cannot measure his distance with his eye, he cannot do it with all the folding elevating sights that can be made. One of the principal things in shooting is, for a man to measure his distance before he shoots, and if he cannot do it, all the sights that can be added will not make him a good shot; this is only to be obtained by practice.

A rifleman should fire from a rest at a short distance, first, to ascertain the straight line of his sights; after he has so done, he should ascertain the elevation of his rifle at point blank. From that he will elevate or depress according to the distance he is from the object he fires at. The sights on the king's regulation rifles, are intended for 200 yards point blank.

A rifleman should not be in too great a hurry in loading and firing; I have found one shot in one minute as much as I could fire to keep myself steady. In ramming down the ball the air will sometimes force the powder into the touch-hole very hard, which will occasion the rifle to hang fire or flash in the pan, and not fire the powder in the barrel, particularly in joint or patent breech barrels; as the narrow chamber at the bottom of breech inside, is forced full of powder so hard, by the air which the ball drives before it; it makes the rifle hang or misfire more than it will with the plain breech. This I have frequently experienced, and for which reason I give the preference to plain breech's to rifle barrels.

A rifle to hang or misfire, is a great denial to a rifleman, and may be the cause of his losing his life. To remedy this, put a picker made for that purpose, into the touch-hole whilst loading; shut down the hammer on the picker or the air will blow it out; when loaded, take out the picker, prime, and with the picker force a little powder into the touch-hole. Be careful not to prime too full, as it will prevent the hammer going down, and occasion the prime to be lost, or the damp to get to the priming; which will make the rifle hang or misfire, a pin or small feather will answer to stop the touch-hole occasionally. This mode of loading will do in practice, but in action, I have my doubts, as they will be apt to loose the picker; in lieu of a picker or feather after loading, prick the touch-hole; this will loosen the powder which is forced hard in loading.

A rifleman should be careful not to have his lock on full cock whilst loading, as from the pressure of forcing down the ball it might go off, which might be attended with bad consequences. To clean a barrel after firing, wash the barrel out with hot or cold water, which can be most conveniently got; after drying the barrel with tow, put a little sweet-oil on the tow, rub it up and down the barrel; the muzzle of the barrel should be stopped to keep out the air to prevent rust, or it will soon injure the rifles.

A rifle barrel should be always kept brown, as it will prevent the glare of the sun obstructing the eye, as is the case on all bright barrels. I have here added four different positions, the most easy and certain way which I could find to fire in, as per figures, No, 1, 2, 3, 4. Likewise two men targets that I have fired at, and a table of the weight and diameter of lead balls, from one to fifty to the pound. The charge of good powder I have found to be nearly equal to one-third the weight of the ball, priming included.

A rifleman should not blame his rifle if it does not at all times throw the ball to one point, I have seen rifles fixed so as to be immovable in firing, and yet have heard, as here shewn in appendix, No. 1, 2, and 3, and many other experiments that I have attended, and have had the same effect, although every care has been taken in loading, &c. The breech and barrel should be marked on the top with an index, to shew when the breech pin in barrel is turned to its right mark; that will at all times keep the sight and touch-hole in the right place.

I have recommended to the Honourable Board of Ordnance, to have all the musquets marked so, which they have been pleased to adopt; that will enable the soldiers to see when the pins are right, and prevent many mistakes that have before happened, by their turning the breech-pin in barrel too far, or not far enough; that has thrown the touch-hole out of its place, either under the pan or over the hammer, which has been one cause of the musquets frequently missing fire; and it will bring the loops on barrel, to their right place, which will prevent the stock from being split; that as often been the case, by the loops not being in their right place to receive the bolts or wire pins that hold the barrel in the stock.

It was ever understood, that ¾ or a whole turn in the angle of rifle, in a barrel three feet in length, was the best for throwing a ball to a certainty; this mode of rifling is practised by the Germans, French, and Americans, and all the foreign rifles that I have ever yet seen are rifled so, and several English gun makers, are firmly of opinion, that one turn in four feet is the best angle possible.

In the year 1800, many of the gun makers in England, were called on by the Honourable Board of Ordnance, to produce a specimen, in order to get the best rifle possible; among the rest I was one; there was also many rifles from the Continent and America all tried at Woolwich, by a committee of field officers appointed for that purpose, for the use of a rifle corps, raised by government; my barrel having ¼ turn only in the rifle, was approved of in preference to the whole; the practice of which is here shewn, as per appendix No. 1, fired at a target 300 yards distance. In the year 1803, a target fired at 200 yards distance, by order of His Royal Highness the Prince of Wales, with a rifle barrel 20 inches in length, for the use of his regiment of light dragoons.

The experiment was carried out by order of the Honourable Board of Ordnance.

The 4th day of February. 1800.

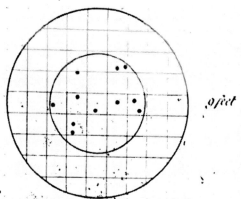

0 feet

This Barrel made by Mr Baker two feet six in length, quarter turn in rifle was only fixed in a mortar bed as was all the other rifle barrels fixed on these experiments in such a manner as to be perfectly immoveable; 12 rounds were fired a target 300 yards distance 11 of which struck as points here shewn the balls are the same that are used in mosquets, 14½ of which weigh a pound with four rums of powder; the balls were placed in a greased leather patch. After firing many reign rifles as well as English, this had the preference of the whole.

Sign'd .... Thomas Bloomfield.
Colonel & Inspector of Royal Artillery

in Norwich, March 5 ...
PREMIX, N°. II. —————————————————————————— APPENDIX, N° III.

his Experiment was by order of his ROYAL HIGHNESS the PR. of WALES... June 4.1803.

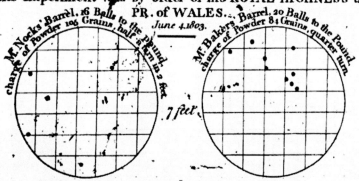

Mr Nocks' Barrel. 16 Balls to the Pound charge of Powder 106 Grains, half a turn in 2 feet

Mr Bakers Barrel. 20 Balls to the Pound charge of Powder 84 Grains, quarter turn.

7 feet

The two barrels 20 inches in length were fired at a target 200 yards distance. firmly fixed in a mortar bed in such a manner as to be perfectly immoveable; rounds from each barrel were fired, and points struck as in targets here shewn. Bakers barrel was afterwards mounted in a stock & 18 rounds were fired by m from the shoulder, without a rest, at a target 100 yards distance with balls to the pound fixed to the cartridge as in use for smooth barrels; in rather less than seven minutes, 15 of which struck the target; the extreme divergence of the balls in inches is 22 to the right, 29½ to the left 35½ over and 25 inches under.

Sign'd   Benjamin Bloomfield

Weight of Lead Balls from One to Fifty to the Pound.
16 Ounces a Pound, 16 Drams an Ounce, 28 Grains a Dram.

By Ezekiel Baker, No. 24 White Chapel Road.

DIAMETERS.

Numb. of Balls	Ounces	Drams	Grains	Numb.	Inch.	8	10	16	20	28	32	40	50	64	80	100	150
1	16			1	1	5		1									
2	8			2	1	2		1			1						
3	5	5	9 1/3	3	1	1										1	
4	4			4	1			1									
5	3	3	5 3/5	5		7		1							1		
6	2	10	18 2/3	6		7						1					
7	2	4	16	7		7										1	
8	2			8		6		1					1				
9	1	12	12 4/9	9		6									1		1
10	1	9	16 4/5	10		6										1	1
11	1	7	7 1/11	11		6											1
12	1	5	9 1/3	12		5		1						1			
13	1	3	22 4/13	13		5		1							1		
14	1	2	8	14		5		1									1
15	1	1	1 13/15	15		5				1							1
16	1			16		5					1						1
17		15	1 11/17	17		5						1					
18		14	6 1/9	18		5							1				
19		13	13 1/19	19		5											
20		12	22 2/5	20		4	1								1		
21		12	5 7/21	21		4	1										1
22		11	17 5/11	22		4		1						1			
23		11	3 13/23	23		4		1							1		1
24		10	18 2/3	24		4		1				1					
25		10	6 18/25	25		4		1								1	
26		9	23 8/13	26		4		1									
27		9	13 13/27	27		4			1								1
28		9	4	28		4			1								
29		8	23 5/29	29		4							2				
30		8	14 14/15	30		4				1							
31		8	7 7/31	31		4					1						
32		8		32		4							1				
33		7	21 7/33	33		4								1			1
34		7	14 14/17	34		4									1		1
35		7	8 8/35	35		4										1	
36		7	3 1/9	36		4											1
37		6	26 27/37	37		4											
38		6	20 13/19	38		3		1			1		1				1
39		6	15 31/39	39		3		1			1		1			1	
40		6	11 1/5	40		3		1			1		1		1		
41		6	6 24/41	41		3		1			1		1				1
42		6	2 4/21	42		3		1			1				1		
43		5	26 30/43	43		3		1			1					1	
44		5	22 10/11	44		3		1			1						1
45		5	18 41/45	45		3		1			1						1×
46		5	15 19/23	46		3		1			1						
47		5	12 24/47	47		3		1					1				
48		5	9 1/3	48		3		1						1			1
49		5	6 24/49	49		3		1						1			

RIFLEMAN PRESENTING

Published by E. Barker, size maker, No 12, White Chapel Road opposite the Church, from Little the Street.

Nº 2.

RIFLEMAN PRESENTING

N.º 9.

Published by I. Barker from number N.º 190 Mile Chapel Road opposite the Church from Little Alie Street.

RIFLEMAN PRESENTING

Published by I. Parker from number N.o 23 New Chapel Street opposite the Church (from whole are sold)

N.o 4.

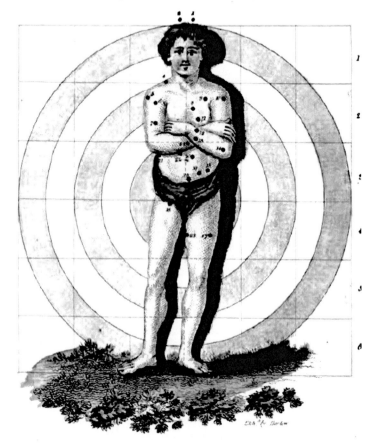

24 Shot at 200 Yards.

Rifle Made and Shot by Ezekiel Baker.

34 Shot at 100 Yards.

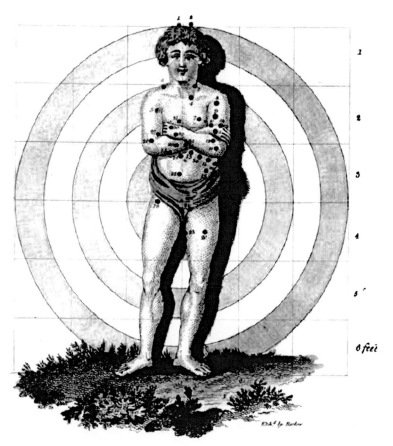

Rifle Made and Shot by Ezekiel Baker.

LEONAUR

ALSO FROM LEONAUR

AVAILABLE IN SOFTCOVER OR HARDCOVER WITH DUST JACKET

THE ART OF WAR *by Antoine Henri Jomini*—Strategy & Tactics From the Age of Horse & Musket.

THE ART OF WAR *by Sun Tzu and Pierre G. T. Beauregard*—*The Art of War* by Sun Tzu and *Principles and Maxims of the Art of War* by Pierre G.T. Beauregard.

THE MILITARY RELIGIOUS ORDERS OF THE MIDDLE AGES *by F. C. Woodhouse*—The Knights Templar, Hospitaller and Others.

THE BENGAL NATIVE ARMY *by F. G. Cardew*—An Invaluable Reference Resource.

ARTILLERY THROUGH THE AGES—*by Albert Manucy*—A History of the DEvelopment and Use of Cannons, Mortars, Rockets & Projectiles from Earliest Times to the Nineteenth Century.

THE SWORD OF THE CROWN *by Eric W. Sheppard*—A History of the British Army to 1914.

THE 7TH (QUEEN'S OWN) HUSSARS: Volume 3—1818-1914 *by C. R. B. Barrett*—On Campaign During the Canadian Rebellion, the Indian Mutiny, the Sudan, Matabeleland, Mashonaland and the Boer War Volume 3: 1818-1914.

THE CAMPAIGN OF WATERLOO *by Antoine Henri Jomini*—A Political & Military History from the French perspective.

THE AUXILIA OF THE ROMAN IMPERIAL ARMY *by G. L. Cheeseman.*

RIFLE & DRILL *by S. Bertram Browne*—The Enfield Rifle Musket, 1853 and the Drill of the British Soldier of the Mid-Victorian Period *A Companion to the New Rifle Musket* and *A Practical Guide to Squad and Setting-up Drill.*

NAPOLEON'S MEN AND METHODS *by Alexander L. Kielland*—The Rise and Fall of the Emperor and His Men Who Fought by His Side.

THE WOMAN IN BATTLE *by Loreta Janeta Velazquez*—Soldier, Spy and Secret Service Agent for the Confederancy During the American Civil War.

THE MILITARY SYSTEM OF THE ROMANS *by Albert Harkness.*

THE BATTLE OF ORISKANY 1777 *by Ellis H. Roberts*—The Conflict for the Mowhawk Valley During the American War of Independenc.

PERSONAL RECOLLECTIONS OF JOAN OF ARC *by Mark Twain.*

LEONAUR

ALSO FROM LEONAUR
AVAILABLE IN SOFTCOVER OR HARDCOVER WITH DUST JACKET

FARAWAY CAMPAIGN *by F. James*—Experiences of an Indian Army Cavalry Officer in Persia & Russia During the Great War.

REVOLT IN THE DESERT *by T. E. Lawrence*—An account of the experiences of one remarkable British officer's war from his own perspective.

MACHINE-GUN SQUADRON *by A. M. G.*—The 20th Machine Gunners from British Yeomanry Regiments in the Middle East Campaign of the First World War.

A GUNNER'S CRUSADE *by Antony Bluett*—The Campaign in the Desert, Palestine & Syria as Experienced by the Honourable Artillery Company During the Great War .

DESPATCH RIDER *by W. H. L. Watson*—The Experiences of a British Army Motorcycle Despatch Rider During the Opening Battles of the Great War in Europe.

TIGERS ALONG THE TIGRIS *by E. J. Thompson*—The Leicestershire Regiment in Mesopotamia During the First World War.

HEARTS & DRAGONS *by Charles R. M. F. Crutwell*—The 4th Royal Berkshire Regiment in France and Italy During the Great War, 1914-1918.

INFANTRY BRIGADE: 1914 *by John Ward*—The Diary of a Commander of the 15th Infantry Brigade, 5th Division, British Army, During the Retreat from Mons.

DOING OUR 'BIT' *by Ian Hay*—Two Classic Accounts of the Men of Kitchener's 'New Army' During the Great War including *The First 100,000 & All In It*.

AN EYE IN THE STORM *by Arthur Ruhl*—An American War Correspondent's Experiences of the First World War from the Western Front to Gallipoli-and Beyond.

STAND & FALL *by Joe Cassells*—With the Middlesex Regiment Against the Bolsheviks 1918-19.

RIFLEMAN MACGILL'S WAR *by Patrick MacGill*—A Soldier of the London Irish During the Great War in Europe including *The Amateur Army, The Red Horizon & The Great Push*.

WITH THE GUNS *by C. A. Rose & Hugh Dalton*—Two First Hand Accounts of British Gunners at War in Europe During World War 1- Three Years in France with the Guns and With the British Guns in Italy.

THE BUSH WAR DOCTOR *by Robert V. Dolbey*—The Experiences of a British Army Doctor During the East African Campaign of the First World War.

LEONAUR

ALSO FROM LEONAUR
AVAILABLE IN SOFTCOVER OR HARDCOVER WITH DUST JACKET

THE 9TH—THE KING'S (LIVERPOOL REGIMENT) IN THE GREAT WAR 1914 - 1918 *by Enos H. G. Roberts*—Mersey to mud—war and Liverpool men.

THE GAMBARDIER *by Mark Severn*—The experiences of a battery of Heavy artillery on the Western Front during the First World War.

FROM MESSINES TO THIRD YPRES *by Thomas Floyd*—A personal account of the First World War on the Western front by a 2/5th Lancashire Fusilier.

THE IRISH GUARDS IN THE GREAT WAR - VOLUME 1 *by Rudyard Kipling*—Edited and Compiled from Their Diaries and Papers—The First Battalion.

THE IRISH GUARDS IN THE GREAT WAR - VOLUME 1 *by Rudyard Kipling*—Edited and Compiled from Their Diaries and Papers—The Second Battalion.

ARMOURED CARS IN EDEN *by K. Roosevelt*—An American President's son serving in Rolls Royce armoured cars with the British in Mesopatamia & with the American Artillery in France during the First World War.

CHASSEUR OF 1914 *by Marcel Dupont*—Experiences of the twilight of the French Light Cavalry by a young officer during the early battles of the great war in Europe.

TROOP HORSE & TRENCH *by R.A. Lloyd*—The experiences of a British Life-guardsman of the household cavalry fighting on the western front during the First World War 1914-18.

THE EAST AFRICAN MOUNTED RIFLES *by C.J. Wilson*—Experiences of the campaign in the East African bush during the First World War.

THE LONG PATROL *by George Berrie*—A Novel of Light Horsemen from Gallipoli to the Palestine campaign of the First World War.

THE FIGHTING CAMELIERS *by Frank Reid*—The exploits of the Imperial Camel Corps in the desert and Palestine campaigns of the First World War.

STEEL CHARIOTS IN THE DESERT *by S. C. Rolls*—The first world war experiences of a Rolls Royce armoured car driver with the Duke of Westminster in Libya and in Arabia with T.E. Lawrence.

WITH THE IMPERIAL CAMEL CORPS IN THE GREAT WAR *by Geoffrey Inchbald*—The story of a serving officer with the British 2nd battalion against the Senussi and during the Palestine campaign.

Lightning Source UK Ltd.
Milton Keynes UK
UKOW052214150312

189009UK00001B/30/P